Made To Lead: A Guide Against Gangs For At Risk Youth

James Hardy

Published by Dynasty Publications, 2024.

MADE TO LEAD: A GUIDE AGAINST GANGS FOR AT RISK YOUTH

First edition. October 23, 2024.

Written by James Hardy.

All Praises To The Most High. Without You I Would Be Nothing.

Dedicated To The Lost & The Forgotten. Where There Is A Will There Is A Way. & It's Never Too Late.

To The Youth. You Are The Future. You Where Made To Lead!

Introduction

My name is James Hardy, and I'm reaching out to you from a place that many of you know all too well. I come from the same impoverished neighborhoods that you do, and I've walked in the same shoes. I wrote this book to help you navigate through the tumultuous and dangerous times we're living in.

Having experienced the harsh realities of gang life firsthand, I understand the deep wounds it inflicts on our people and our communities. Gangs don't just ruin lives—they devastate homes, tear apart families, and extinguish dreams. I began my journey into gang life at just 13 years old, embarking on a reckless path that led me to some of the most harrowing experiences imaginable. I lost friends along the way, and eventually, I lost myself. By 17, my involvement in gang activity and various crimes resulted in the loss of my freedom.

Now, at 26, I find myself still bound by the consequences of those choices. Many of the people I started this journey with are gone—either dead, addicted to drugs, or trapped in the same cycle of despair that I now endure. This toxic cycle of gang life only leads to destruction, whether it manifests physically, mentally, spiritually, or all of the above.

I'm here to share my story with you—not just to recount my struggles, but to urge you to consider the choices you face. I beg you to heed the lessons in this book. I believe it has the power to save and transform your lives. Together, we can break the chains that bind us and build a future free from the clutches of gang violence.

May Yahweh bless you all on this journey toward a brighter tomorrow.

Chapter 1: Understanding Gang Culture

Hey there! As we kick off this journey together in Made to Lead: A Guide Against Gangs for At Risk Youth, I want to talk to you about something that might hit close to home—gang culture. I know that many of you may have encountered gangs or have friends who are involved in them. You might even feel the pull to join one, whether it's for a sense of belonging, protection, or respect. In this chapter, we're going to dive deep into the world of gangs—what they are, why they exist, and why they can be so tempting. By understanding these elements, you can better navigate your choices and see that there are other paths available to you.

Defining Gang Culture

Let's start with the basics. What exactly is a gang? A gang is typically a group of people who come together for a common purpose, and unfortunately, that purpose often involves illegal activities. You may see gangs claiming certain neighborhoods, wearing specific colors, or using symbols to identify themselves. It's like a badge of honor to them, but it can come with a lot of baggage.

Gang culture thrives on loyalty and secrecy. Members are expected to follow a set of rules that prioritize the gang above all else. This means loyalty to your crew, readiness to defend your territory, and sometimes engaging in violence against rival gangs. But here's the truth: this so-called loyalty can lead to devastating consequences—not just for you, but for your family and friends.

So, why do young people like you feel attracted to gangs? The reality is, joining a gang can often feel like the only way to find a place where you belong, especially if you're dealing with feelings of isolation or rejection. The idea of being part of something larger than yourself can be incredibly appealing. But as you'll see, that sense of belonging often comes with a heavy price.

Origins of Gang Culture

Let's take a step back and look at where gangs came from. The roots of gang culture go way back—over a century ago. In cities like New York and Chicago, early gangs formed among immigrant communities who were trying to carve out a place for themselves in a new world. They sought belonging and protection, much like you might today. But as time went on, these groups transformed into organized entities focused on crime.

You might wonder how this evolution happened. The truth is, as communities faced challenges such as poverty, lack of jobs, and systemic discrimination, many young people turned to gangs as a means of survival. The history of gang culture is often tied to broader socio-economic issues, which is why it's so important to understand where it all began.

In many cases, gangs offered a sense of identity and purpose to individuals who felt marginalized. They became a way to cope with the harsh realities of life, and for many young people, the gang represented hope for a better future—even if that hope was misguided.

The Appeal of Gang Membership

Now let's talk about why some of you might be drawn to gangs. The appeal can be powerful. Gangs can offer a sense of belonging and community that might be missing in your life. For many young Black youth, feeling isolated or marginalized can make the idea of joining a gang seem like a way to connect with others. It's a way to feel accepted and valued, even if it means joining a life of crime.

You might find that your friends or peers are involved in gangs, and there's a pressure to fit in. The desire to be part of a group can overshadow the potential risks. Think about it: when you see your friends getting recognition and respect within a gang, it's natural to want that same validation. You may think, "If they can do it, so can I." But remember this: that sense of belonging often comes with strings attached. Gangs demand loyalty, and the initiation process can involve violence or illegal activities. You might find yourself caught in a dangerous cycle, doing things you never thought you would just to prove your worth to the gang.

It's essential to recognize that the glamour of gang life is often a facade. Behind the tough exterior, many gang members live in fear—fear of violence, fear of betrayal, and fear of losing their lives or their freedom. The choices you make now can either bind you to this cycle of fear and violence or lead you to a future filled with possibilities.

Socio-Economic Factors Contributing to Gang Culture

Think about your community and the challenges you face. The socio-economic conditions in many neighborhoods—like poverty, a lack of jobs, and failing schools—can make gang life seem like the only option for success. If you feel stuck, it's easy to think that joining a gang is your best bet for financial stability or respect.

In many cases, systemic issues such as racism and discrimination play a significant role in perpetuating gang culture. It's disheartening to see how young Black youth often face barriers to education and employment opportunities. The lack of access to resources can make it feel like joining a gang is the only way to find a sense of power and control in an environment where those things are stripped away.

Many youth are searching for ways to survive, and when there aren't many positive options available, gangs can fill that void. But that's where the cycle begins: without support, without resources, it becomes a vicious loop that's hard to break.

The Role of Media and Pop Culture

Let's not forget the impact of media and pop culture. We live in a world where movies, music, and social media can glamorize gang life. You might see it in music videos that celebrate violence and materialism or in movies that depict gangs as exciting and powerful. This portrayal can warp your view, making gang life seem like an attractive option without showing you the harsh realities behind it.

For instance, hip-hop culture has played a significant role in shaping perceptions of gang life. While many artists tell their stories and reflect their experiences, they sometimes inadvertently glorify the very violence and crime that can destroy lives. It's crucial to recognize that these narratives are not the whole story—they often leave out the pain, loss, and consequences that come with gang involvement.

You might be drawn to the swagger and confidence displayed in these portrayals, thinking that this is what you need to succeed or to be respected. However, the truth is that these images can lead you down a dangerous path. The reality of gang life is filled with heartbreak, loss, and regret, and it's important to see beyond the glamor and recognize the potential consequences of your choices.

The Impact of Gang Culture on Communities

Now, let's talk about the broader impact of gangs on your community. When gangs are present, they don't just affect the individuals involved—they ripple out to everyone. You may notice increased violence, fear, and tension in your neighborhood. Families often feel the need to move away to find safer places, leading to a breakdown of community ties.

The presence of gangs can also lead to heightened police scrutiny, creating a cycle of distrust between law enforcement and community members. Instead of feeling safe, many residents become wary of the very institutions meant to protect them. This creates an environment where it's hard to find positive role models and opportunities, which only feeds into the cycle of gang culture.

When communities are plagued by violence and crime, it can feel like a never-ending struggle. Resources become scarce, and the dreams of young people can be stifled. The weight of these issues can feel overwhelming, but it's crucial to understand that change is possible.

Finding Hope and Alternatives

As we've discussed, the allure of gang culture is understandable, especially when it seems like there are few options. However, it's important to recognize that you have the power to choose a different path. There are countless stories of individuals who have risen above their circumstances and found success without resorting to gang involvement.

It starts with finding your passion—whether it's art, sports, music, or academics. Pursuing your interests can provide you with a sense of purpose and community that doesn't rely on gangs. You have the potential to be a leader in your own right, to inspire others to make positive choices, and to be part of a movement that uplifts your community.

Engaging in community programs, seeking mentorship, and surrounding yourself with positive influences can help steer you away from gangs. Remember that the choices you make today can shape your future. You have the power to break the cycle and create a life filled with opportunities.

Conclusion

So, as we wrap up this chapter, I want you to take a moment and reflect on what we've discussed. Gang culture is not just a distant problem; it's something that affects many of us directly. By understanding the origins, appeal, and socio-economic factors that contribute to gang involvement, you are starting to arm yourself with knowledge—knowledge that can help you make informed choices about your life.

In the upcoming chapters, we will explore the consequences of gang involvement and the power of choice you have in shaping your own future. Remember, you are not alone in this journey. Many have faced similar challenges and have chosen a different path. Together, we can navigate through these complexities and discover that there are brighter, more fulfilling futures awaiting you. The journey toward empowerment begins with understanding—and you're already on your way.

Reflection Questions

1. Have you ever felt drawn to a gang or experienced pressure from peers to join one?

2. What are some positive alternatives you can pursue that align with your interests and passions?

3. How can you build a support network of friends, mentors, and community resources to help you stay away from gangs?

Take some time to think about these questions. The answers you find can guide your decisions and set you on a path toward empowerment and leadership. You have the power to choose your destiny—make it count!

Chapter 2: The Consequences of Gang Involvement

Welcome back! In this chapter of Made to Lead: A Guide Against Gangs for At Risk Youth, we're diving into a topic that is crucial for anyone contemplating gang involvement: the consequences of such a choice. It's easy to get caught up in the allure of gang life—the camaraderie, the power, the respect. But as we explore the realities behind this lifestyle, I want you to understand that the consequences can be devastating, not just for you but for your family and community. By the end of this chapter, I hope you will have a clearer understanding of what it truly means to be involved in a gang and why it's essential to consider the long-term implications of your choices.

Understanding the Immediate Risks

When you think about gangs, the first thing that often comes to mind is violence. It's no secret that gangs can be associated with street fights, shootings, and even murders. This violence isn't just a byproduct of gang culture; it's often a defining feature. As a young person, you may feel invincible and think, "That won't happen to me." But let me tell you: that mindset can lead to serious repercussions.

When you're involved in a gang, you're putting yourself at risk every day. You might be forced to defend your territory, retaliate against rivals, or engage in violent initiation rituals. These situations can escalate quickly and result in severe injuries or even death. Think about it: one moment of anger, one wrong decision, can change your life forever.

Beyond the physical danger, there's also the psychological toll of living in a constant state of fear and paranoia. You might find it hard to trust anyone outside your gang, leading to isolation and a lack of meaningful relationships. This environment can create a cycle of anxiety and stress that follows you everywhere, making it difficult to focus on your future or pursue your dreams.

Legal Consequences

Another significant risk of gang involvement is the legal consequences. Being part of a gang often means engaging in illegal activities, whether it's drug dealing, robbery, or violence. If you get caught, the legal system can hit you hard.

You might think, "I can handle it; I won't get caught." But the truth is, law enforcement is always looking for gang activity. The consequences of getting arrested can be life-altering. A criminal record can limit your job opportunities, impact your ability to pursue higher education, and even affect your relationships.

Many young people end up in juvenile detention centers or adult prisons because of gang-related charges. These experiences can be traumatic and can leave lasting scars. Life in prison is not glamorous; it's a harsh reality filled with violence, loss of freedom, and a struggle for survival. It's essential to understand that the risks you take today can haunt you for years to come.

Impact on Family and Friends

Now, let's talk about the impact of gang involvement on your family and friends. When you choose to join a gang, you're not just affecting yourself; you're also putting your loved ones in danger.

Think about how your decisions ripple out to those around you. Your family may worry constantly about your safety, leading to stress and tension in your home. Parents often feel helpless, fearing for their children's lives while struggling with the realities of gang culture. You may not realize it, but your choices can create a cycle of pain that extends far beyond yourself.

Your friends may also suffer the consequences of your involvement. If you're caught in illegal activities, they could be implicated as well. Loyalty can quickly turn into betrayal, and you might find yourself in situations where trust is broken. The pressure to conform can push friends into dangerous behaviors, resulting in a loss of genuine connections and support.

Community Impact

The consequences of gang involvement extend to the community as well. When gangs are present, they contribute to a culture of violence and fear that can permeate neighborhoods. You may have seen how gang activity leads to increased crime rates, creating an atmosphere where people feel unsafe in their own homes.

Businesses may close, families may move away, and the sense of community can deteriorate. The youth in these neighborhoods are often left with limited options, perpetuating the cycle of gang culture. It becomes a self-fulfilling prophecy: the more violence and crime there is, the more young people feel they need to join gangs for protection or acceptance.

You can be a catalyst for change in your community. By choosing to step away from gang involvement, you can help break the cycle and pave the way for a brighter future for yourself and others. Remember, every choice you make has the power to shape not just your life but the lives of those around you.

Emotional and Psychological Consequences

Let's not forget the emotional and psychological consequences of gang involvement. The lifestyle can lead to feelings of hopelessness, depression, and anxiety. The pressure to conform to gang norms can stifle your individuality, leaving you feeling trapped and disconnected from who you truly are.

You may find yourself in a constant struggle between wanting to belong and yearning for freedom. The fear of violence and betrayal can weigh heavily on your heart, leading to an internal conflict that is hard to reconcile. Many young people in gangs experience trauma, which can have lasting effects on mental health.

Seeking help or finding support can feel difficult, especially in an environment where vulnerability is often seen as weakness. But remember, reaching out for help is a sign of strength. There are professionals, mentors, and community programs ready to support you on your journey to healing and growth. You don't have to face these challenges alone.

Breaking the Cycle: Finding Alternatives

Understanding the consequences of gang involvement is the first step toward making better choices. You have the power to break the cycle and create a future that aligns with your values and aspirations.

So, what can you do instead? Start by exploring your interests and passions. Find activities that inspire you and connect you with positive influences. Whether it's sports, arts, music, or community service, engaging in meaningful pursuits can provide a sense of belonging without the dangers of gang involvement.

Consider seeking mentorship or guidance from individuals who have successfully navigated similar challenges. Many former gang members have turned their lives around and are now dedicated to helping others avoid the pitfalls they faced. Their stories can inspire you and provide valuable insights into how to overcome adversity.

The Power of Community and Support Systems

Building a strong support system is essential as you navigate away from gang culture. Surround yourself with positive role models, mentors, and friends who uplift you. Participate in community programs that promote personal growth and development. Many organizations focus on empowering youth, offering resources and opportunities that can lead to a brighter future.

Your community can be a powerful ally in your journey. Many youth organizations provide mentorship programs, workshops, and resources designed to help you make positive choices. Engage with these resources and connect with others who share your goals and aspirations. Together, you can create a support network that helps you stay on track and pursue your dreams.

Real Stories, Real Choices

To illustrate the realities of gang involvement and the choices you can make, let's consider a few real-life stories of individuals who faced similar challenges.

Story 1: James' Journey

James grew up in a neighborhood where gangs were a common sight. He was drawn to the idea of belonging and protection that a gang seemed to offer. Initially, it felt empowering, and he gained respect among his peers. However, it didn't take long for him to witness the darker side of gang life. He lost friends to violence and faced legal issues that left him with a criminal record.

Eventually, James realized he had to change his life. With the help of a mentor, he redirected his energy into pursuing education and community service. He became involved in programs that focused on empowering youth, sharing his story to help others avoid the mistakes he made. James' journey is a testament to the power of choice and the possibility of redemption.

Story 2: Angela's Transformation

Angela's story is another example of resilience. She faced immense pressure from her peers to join a gang, thinking it would give her the acceptance she craved. However, she watched as her friends became embroiled in violence and legal troubles. Instead of following that path, Angela sought guidance from a teacher who saw her potential.

Through hard work and determination, Angela was able to turn her life around. She became a leader in her community, advocating for youth empowerment and education. Her transformation illustrates that the power to change lies within each of us, regardless of our circumstances.

Conclusion

As we conclude this chapter, I want you to reflect on the consequences of gang involvement and how they can shape your life. The risks are real, and the impact extends beyond yourself to your family, friends, and community. By understanding the potential consequences, you are taking a crucial step toward making informed choices about your future.

Remember, you have the power to break the cycle and choose a different path. Surround yourself with positive influences, seek mentorship, and engage in activities that uplift you. Your story doesn't have to end in gang involvement; it can lead to empowerment, leadership, and success.

As we move forward in this book, we will explore more about the power of choice, resilience, and finding your voice. You are not alone on this journey; together, we can navigate the complexities of life and create a future filled with possibilities. Embrace your potential, and let's take the next step together!

Chapter 3: Finding Your True Path: Identity, Purpose, and Leadership

Welcome back to Made to Lead: A Guide Against Gangs for At Risk Youth. In the previous chapters, we explored the dangerous realities of gang life and the severe consequences that come with those choices. But now, let's pivot to something equally crucial: discovering your identity, understanding your purpose, and embracing your leadership potential.

In this chapter, I want to guide you through the transformative process of finding who you truly are and what you are meant to accomplish in life. Every one of you has a unique story, a distinct set of talents, and the potential to be a leader in your community. But it starts with self-discovery. By understanding yourself and your passions, you can carve out a path that leads to fulfillment and success, far away from the lure of gang culture.

Understanding Identity: Who Are You?

To begin this journey, let's explore the concept of identity. Your identity is composed of your values, beliefs, experiences, and aspirations. It's who you are at your core. In a world filled with influences—friends, media, and societal expectations—finding your true identity can feel overwhelming. You might feel pressured to conform to certain roles or behaviors that don't align with your true self.

Self-Reflection Exercise:

Take a moment to reflect on the following questions:

1. What are my values? Consider what matters most to you. Is it family, education, respect, community, or something else? Write these down and think about why they resonate with you.

2. What are my interests and passions? Think about what excites you, what activities make you lose track of time, and what subjects you enjoy learning about. Perhaps you love drawing, playing sports, or exploring technology. Make a list and highlight those that spark joy.

3. What are my strengths and weaknesses? Recognize your unique talents and areas for improvement. This self-awareness will help you grow. Don't be afraid to ask trusted friends or family members for their perspectives on your strengths; sometimes, they see greatness in you that you may overlook.

4. What are my dreams and aspirations? Envision your future. What do you want to achieve? What legacy do you want to leave behind? Write down your goals, no matter how big or small, and think about the steps necessary to reach them.

Writing down your thoughts can be an effective way to process these questions. This self-reflection will help you gain clarity about who you are and what you want to accomplish.

The Importance of Purpose

Once you have a better understanding of your identity, it's essential to consider your purpose. Purpose is the reason you wake up every morning; it's what drives you to pursue your passions and dreams. A clear sense of purpose can be a powerful motivator, guiding your decisions and keeping you on track, especially during challenging times.

Finding Your Purpose:

To identify your purpose, consider the following:

What problems do I want to solve? Think about issues in your community or the world that resonate with you. How can your unique skills and experiences contribute to positive change? Perhaps it's addressing educational inequities or advocating for mental health awareness.

How do I want to impact others? Reflect on the kind of legacy you want to leave. Do you want to inspire others, provide support, or create opportunities for those who need it? Write down specific ways you want to make a difference, and consider how those align with your values.

What makes me feel fulfilled? Pay attention to the activities and experiences that bring you joy and satisfaction. These can offer clues about your purpose. It could be through volunteering, mentoring others, or pursuing a creative outlet that allows you to express yourself.

When you align your actions with your purpose, you'll find a deeper sense of fulfillment. Your purpose will serve as a compass, guiding you away from destructive influences and towards a life of meaning and significance.

Embracing Leadership: You Are a Leader

As you begin to uncover your identity and purpose, it's essential to recognize your leadership potential. Leadership isn't just about authority or position; it's about influence, inspiration, and taking responsibility for yourself and others. Each of you has the capacity to be a leader in your own right, regardless of your circumstances.

Types of Leadership:

Consider the following types of leadership:

1. Personal Leadership: This involves leading yourself—making positive choices, setting goals, and holding yourself accountable. Personal leadership lays the foundation for influencing others. It requires discipline, self-reflection, and the courage to act according to your values.

2. Peer Leadership: As a peer leader, you can inspire and motivate those around you. Your actions and choices can encourage your friends to make positive decisions. Consider how you can support your peers in making healthy choices, whether it's advocating for education over violence or fostering creativity through art.

3. Community Leadership: This involves taking action to improve your community. Whether it's through volunteering, organizing events, or advocating for change, community leadership empowers you to make a difference. Look for opportunities in your neighborhood where you can engage with local initiatives or participate in community service.

4. Visionary Leadership: Visionary leaders have the ability to see beyond the present and inspire others to work towards a common goal. By articulating a clear vision, you can rally support and create positive change. Think about what you want to achieve, and share that vision with others to create a collective movement.

The Power of Influence

Your influence as a leader can have a significant impact on those around you. Every choice you make sends a message, and your actions can inspire others to follow suit. When you lead by example, you create a ripple effect that can extend far beyond your immediate circle.

The Responsibility of Leadership:

With leadership comes responsibility. As you embrace your role as a leader, remember that your choices affect not just you, but also your family, friends, and community. This realization can motivate you to make choices that align with your values and purpose.

Understanding Your Influence:

Be Authentic: Authenticity breeds trust. When you are true to yourself and your values, others are more likely to respect you and be influenced by your actions. Share your struggles and successes honestly, and don't be afraid to show vulnerability.

Lead with Empathy: Understand the struggles and challenges faced by others. Empathetic leaders can connect with their peers on a deeper level, creating a sense of community and support. Take time to listen to others' stories; this will not only strengthen your relationships but also enhance your leadership skills.

Stay Committed: Leadership requires commitment. It's essential to stay dedicated to your goals, even when faced with obstacles. Your perseverance can inspire others to do the same. Remember, it's okay to stumble along the way; what matters is how you get back up and continue to move forward.

Building Your Support System

As you embark on this journey of self-discovery and leadership, remember that you don't have to do it alone. Surrounding yourself with a supportive network can significantly enhance your growth and success.

Identifying Supportive Relationships:

Look for mentors, friends, and family members who uplift and encourage you. Seek out individuals who share your values and aspirations. They can provide guidance, support, and accountability as you pursue your goals.

Mentorship: Find a mentor who can offer wisdom and insight based on their own experiences. A mentor can help you navigate challenges and provide valuable advice. Look for someone you respect and admire, and don't hesitate to reach out to them.

Peer Support: Connect with peers who share your interests and ambitions. Having a supportive group of friends can motivate you and create a positive environment for growth. Organize study groups, collaborate on projects, or participate in activities that strengthen your bond.

Community Programs: Engage in community programs that promote leadership development. Many organizations offer workshops, resources, and networking opportunities designed to empower youth. Research local programs that align with your interests and get involved.

Overcoming Obstacles on Your Journey

Every journey has its obstacles. As you work towards discovering your identity and purpose, you may encounter challenges that test your resolve. It's essential to remember that setbacks are a natural part of growth.

Building Resilience:

Resilience is the ability to bounce back from adversity. Developing resilience can help you navigate obstacles and stay focused on your goals. Here are some strategies to build resilience:

1. Stay Positive: Focus on the positive aspects of your journey, and practice gratitude. A positive mindset can help you overcome challenges and maintain motivation. Create a gratitude journal where you write down things you are thankful for each day.

2. Learn from Failure: Instead of viewing failure as a setback, see it as an opportunity for growth. Analyze what went wrong and identify lessons you can apply in the future. Remember that every successful person has faced failures; it's how you respond to them that matters.

3. Seek Support: When facing challenges, don't hesitate to reach out for help. Lean on your support system and share your struggles with trusted individuals. Opening up can lighten your emotional load and provide new perspectives on your situation.

4. Set Realistic Goals: Break your goals into manageable steps. This will help you stay motivated and make progress, even when faced with obstacles. Celebrate your small victories along the way; they'll fuel your momentum.

Real Stories of Transformation

To further illustrate the journey of self-discovery and leadership, let's explore a couple of inspiring stories of young people who found their paths and made a difference.

Story 1: Malik's Transformation

Malik grew up in a neighborhood plagued by gang violence. He was drawn into that lifestyle, believing it was his only option. However, after witnessing the devastating impact of gang involvement on his friends and family, he decided to turn his life around. With the help of a mentor at his school, he began to explore his interests in music and community service.

Malik's mentor encouraged him to use his passion for music as a platform for positive change. He started writing lyrics that addressed the challenges faced by youth in his community, promoting messages of hope and resilience. With each song, Malik not only found a way to express himself but also inspired others to reconsider their paths. His music reached a wider audience through local events, where he performed in front of his peers, encouraging them to choose alternatives to gang life.

Through his journey, Malik discovered his true identity as an artist and a leader. He realized that his purpose was to uplift others and spark conversations about the issues affecting his community. By staying true to himself and surrounding himself with supportive peers, Malik transformed from a potential gang member into a role model for those around him.

Story 2: Jamila's Journey

Jamila faced a different set of challenges. Growing up, she struggled with low self-esteem and often felt overlooked. Although she had a talent for art, she lacked the confidence to pursue it. One day, she attended a community workshop focused on empowering young women. The experience opened her eyes to the strength within her and inspired her to embrace her creativity.

Jamila began to paint murals that conveyed messages of empowerment and resilience. Her art became a visual representation of her journey and the struggles faced by many young Black women in her community. As she gained recognition for her work, she also became involved in youth mentorship programs, sharing her story with others who might be struggling with their self-identity.

Through her art, Jamila not only found her voice but also became a beacon of hope for young girls around her. She showed them that they could rise above their circumstances and embrace their unique talents. Jamila's journey demonstrates the power of self-discovery and the impact that one person can have on their community.

Your Path Forward

As we conclude this chapter, I want you to reflect on your own journey of self-discovery. Remember, your identity, purpose, and leadership potential are waiting to be uncovered. Embrace the process of finding who you are and what you are meant to achieve. Each of you has the power to shape your destiny and positively influence the lives of those around you.

1. Take Action: Start implementing the self-reflection exercises discussed earlier. Spend time each week journaling about your thoughts and experiences. Allow yourself to evolve as you gain new insights.

2. Set Goals: Create short-term and long-term goals that align with your values and purpose. Write them down and keep track of your progress. Celebrate your achievements, no matter how small.

3. Seek Opportunities: Look for community programs, workshops, or events that can enhance your leadership skills. Surround yourself with individuals who inspire you and share your ambitions.

4. Stay Committed: Your journey may have ups and downs, but remember to stay committed to your path. Surround yourself with positivity and resilience, and never hesitate to seek support when needed.

5. Lead by Example: As you begin to uncover your identity and embrace your leadership potential, remember to lead by example. Your choices can inspire others to make positive changes in their lives.

Conclusion

You are capable of achieving great things, and the path to realizing your full potential begins with understanding who you are and what you want to achieve. In a world that often tries to pull you in different directions, remember that you were made to lead. By embracing your identity, purpose, and leadership potential, you can forge a path that not only transforms your life but also uplifts those around you.

In the next chapter, we will dive deeper into practical strategies for building resilience and navigating challenges as you continue your journey. Remember, every leader faces obstacles, but it's how you respond to those challenges that defines your success. Keep pushing forward—you have the power to create the life you desire and inspire others to do the same.

Chapter 4: Building Resilience: Overcoming Challenges and Staying Strong

Welcome back to Made to Lead: A Guide Against Gangs for At Risk Youth. In the previous chapters, we explored the importance of understanding your identity, discovering your purpose, and embracing your leadership potential. Now, we're going to tackle a critical aspect of your journey: resilience.

Life is full of challenges, and the path you choose is not always easy. You will face obstacles, setbacks, and moments of doubt. However, resilience—the ability to bounce back from adversity—will be your greatest ally as you navigate the complexities of life. In this chapter, we will explore what resilience is, why it matters, and how you can develop this essential skill to stay strong in the face of challenges.

Understanding Resilience

Resilience is not just about enduring hardships; it's about thriving despite them. It's the capacity to adapt to difficult circumstances, learn from failures, and emerge stronger than before. Resilient individuals don't let setbacks define them; instead, they view challenges as opportunities for growth.

The Components of Resilience:

1. Emotional Awareness: Understanding your emotions is a crucial aspect of resilience. When faced with adversity, you may experience a range of feelings, including anger, sadness, or frustration. Acknowledging these emotions without judgment allows you to process them effectively and avoid being overwhelmed.

2. Positive Mindset: Resilient individuals maintain a positive outlook even in challenging situations. This doesn't mean ignoring the difficulties; rather, it's about focusing on what you can control and finding silver linings. A positive mindset helps you approach problems with creativity and optimism.

3. Problem-Solving Skills: Resilience involves actively seeking solutions rather than dwelling on problems. Developing strong problem-solving skills enables you to assess situations, identify options, and implement effective strategies to overcome obstacles.

4. Social Support: Building a support network is vital for resilience. Surrounding yourself with positive influences—friends, family, mentors—provides emotional support and practical advice when you need it most. These connections can help you feel less isolated during tough times.

5. Self-Compassion: Being kind to yourself is essential for resilience. Recognize that everyone makes mistakes and faces challenges. Instead of criticizing yourself for perceived failures, practice self-compassion by acknowledging your efforts and understanding that setbacks are a natural part of growth.

The Importance of Resilience

Resilience is particularly important for young people, especially in communities where systemic challenges, violence, and negative influences can feel overwhelming. Developing resilience equips you with the tools to navigate these difficulties and emerge stronger.

Why Resilience Matters:

Coping with Adversity: Life is unpredictable. You will encounter obstacles that test your strength and determination. Resilience helps you cope with challenges effectively, allowing you to bounce back and continue pursuing your goals.

Fostering Personal Growth: Every setback presents an opportunity for growth. Resilience encourages you to learn from your experiences, adapt your approach, and develop new skills. The lessons learned during difficult times often lead to greater self-awareness and personal development.

Enhancing Mental Well-Being: Resilience is closely linked to mental health. Individuals with strong resilience are better equipped to manage stress and anxiety. They're less likely to succumb to feelings of helplessness or despair, promoting overall emotional well-being.

Promoting Success: Resilience is a key factor in achieving your goals. Those who are resilient tend to persevere in the face of challenges, making them more likely to succeed in their endeavors. Your ability to navigate setbacks will determine how far you can go in pursuing your dreams.

Cultivating Resilience: Practical Strategies

Now that we've established the importance of resilience, let's explore practical strategies you can implement in your life to build and strengthen this essential skill.

1. Develop a Growth Mindset

A growth mindset is the belief that your abilities and intelligence can be developed through dedication and hard work. Adopting a growth mindset encourages you to view challenges as opportunities for learning rather than insurmountable obstacles. Here's how to cultivate a growth mindset:

Embrace Challenges: Instead of avoiding difficult tasks, approach them with curiosity and enthusiasm. Understand that challenges are opportunities to grow.

Learn from Criticism: Rather than viewing feedback as a personal attack, consider it an opportunity for improvement. Constructive criticism can help you refine your skills and grow as a leader.

Celebrate Effort: Recognize the value of hard work. Focus on the effort you put into your tasks, regardless of the outcome. Celebrate your dedication and commitment to growth.

Visualize Success: Spend time imagining yourself overcoming challenges and achieving your goals. Visualization can help create a positive mindset, preparing you for success.

2. Build Emotional Intelligence

Emotional intelligence is the ability to understand and manage your emotions and the emotions of others. Developing emotional intelligence can enhance your resilience by enabling you to navigate challenging situations effectively. Here are some ways to improve your emotional intelligence:

Practice Self-Reflection: Take time to reflect on your emotions and reactions. Journaling can help you process your feelings and gain insights into your emotional patterns. Ask yourself questions like, "What emotions did I experience today?" and "How did I respond to them?"

Identify Triggers: Pay attention to situations that evoke strong emotional responses. Understanding your triggers allows you to prepare for and manage your reactions. For example, if you know that certain environments or conversations trigger stress, plan ahead to minimize your exposure to those triggers.

Enhance Empathy: Cultivate empathy by actively listening to others and trying to understand their perspectives. Empathy strengthens your relationships and fosters a sense of connection, which is crucial for resilience. Practice putting yourself in someone else's shoes to appreciate their feelings and experiences.

Practice Active Listening: When someone shares their feelings with you, listen attentively without interrupting. Show that you value their perspective by responding thoughtfully.

3. Establish Strong Relationships

Building a support network is vital for resilience. Surround yourself with individuals who uplift and encourage you. Here's how to establish and nurture strong relationships:

Seek Mentors: Identify individuals who inspire you and who can offer guidance. Mentors can provide valuable insights and support during challenging times. Look for teachers, community leaders, or family members who can help you navigate life's complexities.

Communicate Openly: Foster open and honest communication with your friends and family. Share your struggles and successes, and encourage them to do the same. Establishing a culture of trust within your relationships allows you to seek help when needed.

Engage in Community Activities: Participate in community events, clubs, or organizations that align with your interests. Building connections within your community can provide a strong support system. Volunteering is an excellent way to meet like-minded individuals and develop a sense of belonging.

Offer Support to Others: Resilience is a two-way street. When you support others, you strengthen your relationships and create a network of mutual encouragement.

4. Develop Problem-Solving Skills

Effective problem-solving is a crucial component of resilience. The ability to analyze situations and identify solutions empowers you to overcome obstacles. Here's how to enhance your problem-solving skills:

Define the Problem: Take time to clearly articulate the issue you're facing. Understanding the problem is the first step toward finding a solution. Ask yourself, "What exactly is the problem, and how does it affect me?"

Brainstorm Solutions: Generate a list of potential solutions without judgment. Allow your creativity to flow and consider various perspectives. Involve friends or mentors in the brainstorming process to gain new insights.

Evaluate Options: Assess the pros and cons of each solution. Consider factors such as feasibility, potential outcomes, and alignment with your values. Ask yourself, "What are the possible consequences of each option?"

Take Action: Choose the solution that seems most viable and take action. Implementing your plan is a crucial step toward overcoming challenges. Remember that action, even small steps, is better than inaction.

Reflect on Outcomes: After implementing your solution, take time to evaluate the outcome. Did it work? What could you do differently next time? This reflection helps you learn from your experiences.

5. Practice Self-Care

Taking care of your physical and mental well-being is essential for resilience. Prioritizing self-care helps you recharge and equips you to face challenges with renewed energy. Here are some self-care practices to consider:

Exercise Regularly: Physical activity releases endorphins, which can improve your mood and reduce stress. Find an exercise routine that you enjoy, whether it's dancing, running, or playing sports. Aim for at least 30 minutes of physical activity most days of the week.

Get Enough Sleep: Prioritize quality sleep to enhance your focus and overall well-being. Establish a bedtime routine that promotes relaxation and restful sleep. Aim for 7-9 hours of sleep each night.

Mindfulness and Meditation: Practicing mindfulness and meditation can help you develop emotional awareness and manage stress. Spend a few minutes each day engaging in mindfulness exercises, such as deep breathing or guided meditation. Apps like Headspace or Calm can help you get started.

Engage in Hobbies: Make time for activities that bring you joy and fulfillment. Pursuing hobbies can provide a sense of accomplishment and boost your overall mood. Whether it's painting, playing music, or cooking, find what inspires you.

Limit Screen Time: Too much screen time can contribute to stress and anxiety. Set boundaries for your use of technology and prioritize real-life interactions and activities that nourish your spirit.

Overcoming Common Challenges

As you work on building your resilience, you may encounter specific challenges that can test your resolve. Let's explore some common obstacles and strategies for overcoming them.

1. Peer Pressure

Peer pressure can be a significant challenge for youth . The desire to fit in and gain acceptance can lead you down paths that compromise your values and goals. Here's how to resist negative peer pressure and maintain your resilience:

Know Your Values: Take time to define your core values. What matters most to you? Having a clear understanding of your values can help you stand firm when faced with pressure to conform. Write them down and refer back to them when you're uncertain.

Surround Yourself with Positive Influences: Seek friendships that uplift and encourage you. Surrounding yourself with peers who share your values and aspirations can help you stay grounded and resilient against negative influences.

Practice Assertiveness: Develop the ability to say "no" when necessary. Assertiveness is not about being confrontational; it's about confidently expressing your boundaries. Practice how to decline invitations or requests that go against your values.

Seek Support: If you feel overwhelmed by peer pressure, talk to someone you trust. A mentor, teacher, or family member can offer guidance and support. They may provide perspectives that help you navigate these challenges effectively.

2. Academic and Personal Pressure

Many young people face immense pressure to succeed academically and personally. This pressure can be overwhelming and lead to anxiety and stress. Here's how to manage academic and personal expectations while maintaining resilience:

Set Realistic Goals: Establish achievable goals that align with your abilities and interests. Break larger goals into smaller, manageable steps. Celebrate your progress along the way to maintain motivation.

Prioritize Time Management: Effective time management can help reduce feelings of overwhelm. Create a schedule that balances your academic responsibilities, extracurricular activities, and self-care. Utilize tools like planners or digital calendars to stay organized.

Practice Self-Compassion: Recognize that nobody is perfect, and mistakes are part of the learning process. Be kind to yourself when facing setbacks or academic challenges. Instead of criticizing yourself, focus on what you can learn from the experience.

Seek Help When Needed: If you're struggling academically or personally, don't hesitate to seek help. Talk to teachers, counselors, or tutors who can provide support and resources. Remember, asking for help is a sign of strength, not weakness.

3. Coping with Loss and Grief

Experiencing loss, whether it's the death of a loved one or the end of a significant relationship, can profoundly impact your resilience. Coping with grief is a personal journey, but there are ways to navigate this difficult experience:

Allow Yourself to Grieve: Understand that grief is a natural response to loss. Allow yourself to feel your emotions fully without judgment. Suppressing your feelings can hinder your healing process.

Connect with Supportive People: Lean on friends, family, or support groups who can provide understanding and comfort during your grieving process. Sharing your feelings with others can be incredibly cathartic.

Create Memorials or Rituals: Consider honoring the memory of your loved one through rituals or memorials. This could involve planting a tree, creating a scrapbook, or participating in activities they enjoyed.

Seek Professional Support: If your grief feels overwhelming or prolonged, consider talking to a counselor or therapist. Professional support can help you process your emotions and develop healthy coping strategies.

Real-Life Stories of Resilience

To illustrate the power of resilience, let's revisit the stories of David and Aaliyah, focusing on the moments that shaped their journeys and the lessons they learned along the way.

David's Journey of Resilience

David's path was not without its challenges. After joining the youth leadership program, he faced skepticism from friends who questioned his commitment. They teased him about spending time in a program that focused on self-improvement, calling him a "try-hard" or a "sellout."

Initially, David felt the sting of their words. He struggled with self-doubt and wondered if he was making the right choice. However, he leaned into the principles of resilience he had started to develop. He reminded himself of his goals and the life he wanted to create for himself.

Instead of distancing himself from his friends, David decided to invite them to join him in the program. He organized a basketball tournament as a way to show them the benefits of the program. Through sports, he highlighted teamwork, discipline, and the importance of making positive choices. His friends began to see the value in what he was doing and eventually joined him.

David's journey taught him that resilience isn't just about personal growth; it's about lifting others up as well. By sharing his experiences and inviting his friends to be part of his journey, he strengthened his relationships and inspired them to consider their paths.

Aaliyah's Artistic Journey

Aaliyah's story was one of courage and determination. As she pursued her passion for art, she faced criticism not just from peers, but also from family members who did not see art as a viable career path. They questioned her commitment to pursuing something that, in their eyes, might not lead to financial stability.

During a particularly challenging period, Aaliyah submitted her artwork to a major exhibition, only to receive a rejection notice. Feeling crushed and disheartened, she contemplated giving up on her dream. However, remembering the resilience she was cultivating, Aaliyah took a step back to reflect on her journey.

Instead of succumbing to defeat, she reached out to her art teacher for advice. Her teacher encouraged her to view rejection as part of the creative process and not a reflection of her talent. Inspired by this perspective, Aaliyah decided to channel her disappointment into a new project—creating a series of pieces that expressed her emotions.

This series, titled Through the Storm, resonated with many, as it depicted themes of struggle, resilience, and hope. When she submitted the series to another exhibition, it received acclaim and opened doors for further opportunities.

Aaliyah learned that resilience involves embracing both success and failure. Her ability to transform setbacks into fuel for her creativity led to greater artistic expression and success.

Your Resilience Toolkit

As you reflect on the stories of David and Aaliyah, consider the following strategies to build your resilience toolkit:

1. Identify Your Strengths: Take time to reflect on your unique strengths and talents. What are you passionate about? Recognizing your strengths can help you navigate challenges more effectively.

2. Practice Flexibility: Life is unpredictable, and plans may change. Cultivating flexibility allows you to adapt to new situations and find alternative solutions when faced with setbacks.

3. Create a Vision Board: Visualize your goals and aspirations by creating a vision board. Include images, quotes, and reminders of what you want to achieve. This visual representation can serve as a powerful motivator during difficult times.

4. Engage in Positive Self-Talk: Replace negative self-talk with affirmations that empower you. Create a list of positive statements about yourself and read them daily to reinforce your self-belief.

5. Seek Professional Help if Needed: If you find yourself struggling with overwhelming emotions or challenges, consider seeking support from a counselor or therapist. They can provide guidance and coping strategies tailored to your needs.

Conclusion

In this chapter, we've explored the concept of resilience and its significance in your journey as a young leader. You have the power to overcome challenges, learn from setbacks, and emerge stronger on the other side. Remember that resilience is a skill you can develop over time through practice and determination.

As you move forward, embrace the strategies we discussed, and remember the stories of David and Aaliyah. Let their experiences inspire you to stay committed to your goals and pursue your passions, even in the face of adversity.

In the next chapter, we will discuss the importance of making positive choices and how to avoid the pitfalls of gang involvement. Your journey to leadership and empowerment continues, and I'm excited to guide you on this path. Together, we'll explore how to create a brighter future for yourself and your community. You were made to lead, and resilience is your key to unlocking your potential.

Chapter 5: The Power of Choice: Navigating Your Path Away from Gangs

As you stand at the crossroads of your life, you will face decisions that will shape your future. Each choice you make is a step toward the life you want to lead or a step toward paths that could lead you away from your goals. In this chapter, I want to talk directly to you about the power of choice and how it can help you navigate away from the temptations and traps of gang involvement. Understanding that you have the ability to make choices—good or bad—will empower you to take control of your life and define your own destiny.

The Reality of Choices

Every day, you are faced with choices, big and small. Some decisions may seem trivial at first, while others feel monumental. The reality is that even the smallest choices can have a significant impact on your life. When it comes to gangs, the decisions you make can determine whether you find yourself on a path toward empowerment or one filled with danger and regret.

Consider, for instance, your choice of friends. Are they individuals who uplift you, inspire you, and encourage you to pursue your goals? Or are they friends who pull you into negative behaviors, influence you to engage in illegal activities, or push you toward gang involvement? The people you surround yourself with can either elevate your life or bring you down. Recognizing this is the first step in understanding the power of choice.

Furthermore, think about how daily habits can become the building blocks of your life. Every time you choose to invest time in studying, practicing a skill, or engaging in positive activities, you are setting the foundation for a successful future. On the flip side, every moment spent in destructive behaviors, such as engaging with gangs or succumbing to peer pressure, can lead to a cycle that is hard to break. Choices create patterns, and patterns become your reality.

Understanding the Allure of Gangs

Before we dive deeper into the power of choice, it's important to understand why gangs are so alluring to many young people. Gangs often promise a sense of belonging, protection, and identity. For those who may feel isolated or marginalized, the camaraderie of a gang can be tempting. You may be drawn to the thrill, the excitement, or the status that gang affiliation can provide.

However, it's crucial to recognize that these promises are often illusions. The reality of gang life is filled with violence, fear, and unpredictability. Gangs thrive on loyalty, but that loyalty can lead to dangerous situations and life-altering consequences. The allure of gangs may be strong, but it is built on a foundation of deception and pain.

Many young people are unaware of the deeper consequences of gang involvement until it's too late. The thrill of the moment can cloud your judgment, making you overlook the long-term impacts on your life, family, and community. When you're in the thick of it, it's easy to get swept away by the excitement and adrenaline, but remember that these feelings are often fleeting. True fulfillment comes from making choices that lead to personal growth, not temporary high.

The Importance of Making Informed Choices

To navigate your path away from gangs, it's essential to understand the choices you face and the consequences that come with them. Knowledge is power, and being informed allows you to make decisions that align with your values and aspirations.

Educate Yourself: Take the time to learn about the realities of gang life. Understand the risks, consequences, and the toll it takes on individuals and communities. Knowledge can empower you to see beyond the allure and make choices that prioritize your well-being. Reading about the stories of those who have left gangs can provide valuable insights into the sacrifices made and the rewards of a different life.

Evaluate Your Options: When faced with a decision, weigh the options. Consider the short-term and long-term effects of each choice. Will it bring you closer to your goals, or will it divert you from your path? Ask yourself how a particular choice aligns with your values and aspirations. Sometimes, taking a moment to pause and reflect can lead you to make a more informed decision.

Seek Guidance: Don't hesitate to seek advice from mentors, teachers, or trusted adults. They can provide perspectives that you might not have considered and help you navigate difficult decisions. Sometimes, an outside perspective can illuminate the best course of action. Remember, asking for help is a sign of strength, not weakness.

Building a Strong Foundation of Choices

As you move forward, it's vital to establish a foundation of positive choices that will guide your journey. Here are some strategies to help you make empowering decisions:

1. Set Clear Goals: Take the time to define your goals and aspirations. What do you want to achieve academically, personally, and professionally? Setting clear goals gives you direction and helps

you make choices that align with your vision for the future. Write these goals down and review them regularly to stay focused.

2. Develop a Decision-Making Process: Create a process for making decisions. When faced with a choice, ask yourself questions like: What are the potential outcomes? How does this decision align with my goals? Am I feeling pressured, or am I making this choice for myself? This structured approach can help you avoid impulsive decisions that you might regret later.

3. Practice Delayed Gratification: Many choices are influenced by the desire for immediate gratification. However, learning to delay gratification can lead to better long-term outcomes. Practice patience and consider the long-term effects of your decisions instead of succumbing to momentary impulses. It might be tempting to seek instant approval or excitement, but remember that lasting fulfillment comes from investing in your future.

4. Surround Yourself with Positive Influences: Your environment plays a significant role in the choices you make. Seek out friendships and relationships that support your goals and values. Positive influences can motivate you to make choices that enhance your life rather than detract from it. Participate in community groups, clubs, or sports teams that foster a sense of belonging without the negativity of gang involvement.

Real-Life Stories: Choices and Consequences

To illustrate the impact of choices, let's explore the stories of two individuals who faced pivotal moments in their lives.

Marcus's Story: A Choice Between Loyalty and Life

Marcus grew up in a neighborhood where gang activity was prevalent. He had friends who were deeply involved in a local gang, and the allure of that lifestyle often tempted him. He wanted to fit in, to feel a sense of belonging that he struggled to find elsewhere.

One day, Marcus was presented with a choice: his friends invited him to participate in a robbery that would earn them quick money and status within the gang. In that moment, Marcus felt torn. On one hand, he craved acceptance and feared being left out; on the other hand, he understood the risks and consequences of his involvement.

He paused and reflected on his aspirations. He wanted to graduate high school, attend college, and create a better life for himself. With those goals in mind, he made a courageous decision—he said no to the robbery. Instead, he chose to speak out against the gang's activities, risking his friendship with those who were involved.

This decision did not come without challenges. Marcus faced backlash from his friends and felt isolated at times. However, he found new allies in teachers and mentors who recognized his potential. They encouraged him to channel his energy into academic pursuits and extracurricular activities. As he distanced himself from gang life, he began to see the rewards of his decision. Marcus became a leader in his school and eventually earned a scholarship to a university, proving that the choice to stand against negative influences was transformative.

Jasmine's Story: Choosing Self-Love Over Acceptance

Jasmine was an exceptionally talented dancer with dreams of making it big in the industry. However, as she navigated her teenage years, she felt the pressure to fit in with a group of friends who engaged in risky behaviors, including drug use and gang affiliation.

At a critical moment, Jasmine was invited to a party where her friends would be experimenting with drugs. She felt torn between her desire to fit in and her passion for dance. In her heart, she knew that choosing to partake in those activities could jeopardize her future.

Instead of attending the party, Jasmine dedicated her time to practice and improve her dancing skills. She sought out local dance classes and became involved in community performances, where she found a supportive network of fellow artists.

As Jasmine pursued her passion, she began to see the rewards of her choice. Her commitment to dance led to opportunities, including auditions and scholarships. Along the way, she also inspired others to prioritize their dreams over the temptations of gang life. Her story serves as a reminder that choosing self-love and authenticity over temporary acceptance can lead to profound fulfillment and success.

Creating Your Path: Steps Toward Empowerment

Now that you've seen how choices can shape lives, it's time to focus on creating your own path away from gangs. Here are actionable steps to help you embrace the power of choice:

1. Identify Your Values: Take time to reflect on what matters most to you. Write down your values, whether they include family, education, community, or personal growth. Let these values guide your decision-making process. Revisit this list periodically to ensure your choices align with what you truly value.

2. Engage in Positive Activities: Seek out activities that align with your passions and interests. Join clubs, sports teams, or community organizations that provide a sense of belonging without the risks associated with gang involvement. Engaging in constructive activities can fill your time with positivity and open doors to new opportunities.

3. Create a Personal Mission Statement: Craft a personal mission statement that encapsulates your goals, values, and aspirations. This statement will serve as a guiding light, helping you stay focused on your path and reminding you of what you stand for. Keep this statement visible—whether it's written on your wall, in your journal, or saved on your phone—to remind yourself of your commitment to making positive choices every day.

4. Build a Support Network: Surround yourself with people who uplift you and share your values. Seek out mentors, friends, and family members who encourage you to pursue your dreams and support your journey away from gangs. A strong support network can help you stay accountable and provide guidance when faced with difficult decisions.

5. Practice Mindfulness: Mindfulness can help you become more aware of your thoughts and feelings, allowing you to make decisions that align with your true self. Take time each day to practice mindfulness through meditation, journaling, or simply

reflecting on your day. This practice can help you remain grounded and make choices that reflect your values and aspirations.

6. Set Small Goals: While big goals are essential, breaking them down into smaller, achievable milestones can make the journey feel less overwhelming. Set short-term goals that lead you closer to your long-term aspirations. Celebrate your achievements, no matter how small, as they reinforce the positive choices you're making.

7. Learn from Mistakes: Understand that everyone makes mistakes. Instead of dwelling on them, use them as learning opportunities. Reflect on what went wrong and how you can make different choices in the future. Growth comes from recognizing that setbacks are part of the journey, not the end of it.

Embracing Your Power

The choices you make today will shape the life you lead tomorrow. Embrace your power to choose, and remember that you have the ability to create a future filled with purpose and potential. As you navigate this journey, remind yourself that your choices reflect who you are and who you aspire to be.

By understanding the allure of gangs, recognizing the importance of informed choices, and taking actionable steps toward positive living, you can carve out a path that leads away from the dangerous temptations of gang life. Your journey may not always be easy, but every decision you make brings you closer to a life of empowerment, fulfillment, and authenticity.

You are capable of achieving great things. The power to choose is in your hands, and you can use it to create a brighter future—not just for yourself, but for your community and the generations to come. Remember, you were made to lead. Embrace that truth and step confidently into your future.

Reflecting on Your Choices

As you finish this chapter, take a moment to reflect on the choices you've made in your life thus far. Write down three choices you are proud of and three choices that you wish had been different. This exercise isn't about guilt; it's about understanding your journey and recognizing that you have the power to learn and grow from every experience.

In your reflection, consider the following questions:

What did I learn from my past choices?

How can I apply these lessons to future decisions?

What steps can I take today to move closer to my goals?

Remember that life is a continuous journey of choices. Each day presents new opportunities to align your actions with your aspirations. Embrace your power to choose, and let that power guide you away from gangs and toward a future filled with hope and promise.

Conclusion: Choosing Your Path

As we move forward in this book, keep the theme of choice in mind. Every chapter will build on the idea that your choices matter. You are in control of your destiny. By understanding the power of choice and making informed decisions, you can steer your life in the direction you desire.

The journey away from gang involvement may be challenging, but it is also filled with opportunities for growth, learning, and self-discovery. You are not alone; there are many others walking a similar path, and together, we can create a community that uplifts and supports one another. Remember, you were made to lead, and the path is yours to forge. Let's take the next step together.

Your Action Steps:

1. Reflect on Your Values: Write down your core values and how they align with your goals.

2. Create Your Mission Statement: Draft a personal mission statement that embodies who you are and what you aspire to be.

3. Identify Supportive Relationships: List three people who inspire you and how they can support your journey away from gangs.

4. Set Short-Term Goals: Outline three small goals you can achieve within the next month that align with your long-term aspirations.

5. Practice Mindfulness: Dedicate time each week to reflect on your choices and how they align with your values and goals.

With each choice you make, you are one step closer to the life you envision for yourself. Remember, you have the power to choose your path, and every choice is a chance to create the future you deserve.

Chapter 6: The Power of Influence: Choosing Role Models and Surroundings

When it comes to avoiding the lure of gangs and shaping your future, few things are more important than who you surround yourself with. In this chapter, I want to dive deep into the concept of influence—how the people, environment, and culture you engage with play a critical role in your journey. We'll explore why it's essential to choose your role models carefully and how the energy of those around you can either push you toward greatness or pull you into dangerous paths.

Understanding Influence: What Shapes Us

From the moment we're born, we're influenced by the world around us. As children, we're shaped by our parents, our family, and our immediate surroundings. We learn language, behavior, and even values from those closest to us. As we grow older, we start to absorb messages from a wider range of sources—friends, media, and the community.

When you're young, it's easy to underestimate just how much these influences matter. You might think, "I'm my own person; I can make my own decisions." And while that's true, it's also important to recognize that your environment, the people you hang with, and the messages you hear on a daily basis profoundly impact your choices.

Let's break it down. Think about the people you spend the most time with. Are they pushing you to be your best self, or are they pulling you toward activities that don't align with who you truly are or where you want to go? Often, we adapt to the energy of the people around us without even realizing it. If you're constantly surrounded by negativity or individuals who glorify destructive lifestyles—such as gang culture—it becomes harder to stay focused on the path you know is right.

But it's not just about avoiding negative influence; it's about seeking out positive ones. Every person you look up to, every mentor, every friend, even the music you listen to and the shows you watch, shapes your mindset. What do you feed your mind? Who are you learning from? These questions matter, and the answers to them are powerful.

Choosing Role Models Wisely

One of the most significant aspects of influence is the role models you choose. For many young people, especially Black youth, finding strong role models can be complicated. The media often highlights the wrong examples, glorifying individuals who have made bad choices or embraced lifestyles that can lead to harm.

However, there are countless positive role models out there—you just need to seek them out. They might not always be in the limelight, but they exist in every community. A role model is someone who represents the type of life you want to live, the values you want to embody, and the type of person you aspire to become.

Let's talk about what to look for in a role model:

1. Values: A true role model lives by principles you admire—whether that's integrity, hard work, kindness, or perseverance. They should represent the qualities that align with your goals, not just superficial success.

2. Resilience: Many of the best role models are individuals who have faced hardship but found a way to rise above it. They didn't take the easy road, and they made mistakes along the way. Their story is about overcoming obstacles, not being trapped by them.

3. Purpose: A great role model has a clear sense of purpose. Whether it's in their career, community work, or personal life, they are driven by something bigger than themselves. This sense of direction can be a powerful motivator for you as you look to craft your own purpose in life.

4. Action-Oriented: True role models don't just talk about their values—they live them. They take action, and their life reflects the choices they make on a daily basis. Watching someone take action toward their goals can inspire you to do the same.

The point is, the role models you choose should help you build a future that you can be proud of. They should make you want to strive for more, not settle for less.

The Impact of Surroundings: Your Environment Shapes Your Destiny

Just as role models are important, the environment you choose to live in can either foster growth or hinder it. Your surroundings include the physical spaces you occupy, the friends you hang with, and even the digital spaces you engage with.

1. Physical Environment: If you live in a neighborhood where gang activity is rampant, it's easy to feel like that's your only option. But remember, you're not a product of your environment—you have the power to shape your destiny. The key is finding ways to distance yourself from negative influences, even if you can't physically leave. This could mean spending time in safe spaces like community centers, libraries, or after-school programs. Your environment should be a place where you feel safe and supported, not one that constantly pulls you toward dangerous behaviors.

2. Social Circles: Who you spend time with matters—probably more than you realize. Think about the five people you talk to the most. Are they pushing you to be better? Are they helping you to stay focused on your goals? Or are they involved in negative behaviors that could drag you down? If you're hanging around people who are part of gangs or who idolize gang culture, it becomes incredibly hard to stay on the right path. On the other hand, surrounding yourself with people who are ambitious, focused, and supportive can keep you motivated and aligned with your goals.

3. Digital Spaces: In today's world, your environment extends beyond the physical. Social media, music, movies, and even video games play a massive role in shaping how we think. Many forms of media glamorize violence, gang life, and materialism, presenting them as exciting or cool. It's important to be mindful of what you consume. Are the things you watch and listen to helping you grow, or are they filling your mind with negative messages? You have the power to choose what you allow into your life, so be intentional about it.

Building a Positive Network

One of the best ways to counter negative influence is by actively building a positive network. A network is more than just a group of friends—it's a community of people who uplift each other, share opportunities, and provide support when needed. Here's how you can start building yours:

1. Seek Out Mentors: Mentors can be older people in your community, teachers, or individuals in professions you're interested in. A mentor offers guidance, support, and real-life advice based on their experiences. They can provide you with valuable insights into how to navigate challenges and make good decisions.

2. Join Positive Groups: There are countless organizations and groups aimed at helping young people stay on the right path. Whether it's a sports team, a church group, a debate team, or a youth leadership organization, these groups offer positive social interactions and a sense of belonging outside of gangs.

3. Support Your Peers: It's not just about what others can do for you—it's also about what you can do for others. Being a positive influence in someone else's life not only helps them but strengthens your own commitment to a better life. If you see a friend struggling with gang pressure, be the one to offer them an alternative. Help them see that there are other ways to succeed.

4. Use Social Media Wisely: Social media can be a powerful tool for connection and learning if used the right way. Follow people who inspire you, who post positive messages, and who can offer you resources and motivation. Block or unfollow accounts that glorify gang life or negativity. Curate your feed to reflect the future you want to create.

Learning to Say No: Setting Boundaries

One of the most powerful tools you can have is the ability to say no. This isn't always easy, especially when peer pressure is involved. But learning to set boundaries is a critical skill for protecting yourself from negative influence.

When someone offers you a path that doesn't align with your values or goals—whether that's gang involvement, drugs, or other destructive behaviors—it's important to recognize that saying no isn't a sign of weakness. It's a sign of strength. It shows that you know your worth and are committed to staying true to yourself.

Setting boundaries might mean distancing yourself from certain people or situations, but it's worth it in the long run. Your peace of mind and your future are too valuable to be compromised by poor decisions.

The Ripple Effect: You Have Influence Too

Never forget that just as you are influenced by others, you also have the power to influence. Whether you realize it or not, your choices, actions, and words impact those around you. If you choose positivity, if you choose growth, if you choose to lead by example, you can inspire your friends, siblings, and community to do the same.

When you decide to break free from the grip of gangs and negative influences, you're not just helping yourself—you're creating a ripple effect that can inspire others to do the same. You have the power to change the culture around you, to uplift others, and to create a new narrative for your community. It starts with you.

Conclusion: Embracing Your Influence

In this chapter, we've explored the power of influence—the role models you choose, the environment you surround yourself with, and the networks you build. Remember, influence is a two-way street. While you are shaped by the world around you, you also have the power to shape it.

Take charge of your surroundings. Be intentional about the people, media, and messages you allow into your life. Seek out mentors, build positive relationships, and take ownership of the role you play in your community. You were made to lead, and part of leadership is recognizing the power of influence—both how it affects you and how you can use it to impact others.

Chapter 7: Breaking the Chains of the Streets: Understanding the True Cost of Gang Life

In this chapter, we are going to have an honest conversation about what gang life really costs. And I'm not just talking about money—though that's part of it. I'm talking about your freedom, your future, your relationships, and your mental well-being. There's a reason why so many people who have been involved in gangs later look back with regret, wishing they had chosen a different path. The streets can give you quick gratification, but they take so much more than they ever give back.

It's easy for young people, especially Black youth, to get drawn into gangs because gangs promise something that is often missing in their lives—respect, money, brotherhood, or protection. But what you have to ask yourself is: At what cost?

The False Promises of Gang Life

One of the main reasons people join gangs is because they feel like it's their only option. Gangs paint themselves as family, offering belonging and support in a world that might otherwise feel hostile or indifferent. This is especially true in communities where opportunities seem limited, and the day-to-day reality is one of struggle. But let's look closer at the promises gangs make and the reality behind them.

1. Respect: Many people join gangs because they want respect. They want to be seen as powerful, untouchable, or feared. But is fear really the same thing as respect? True respect comes from integrity, from being someone who stands on their values, someone who lifts up others, not tears them down. In a gang, the respect

you earn is fragile—based on violence, intimidation, and control. The moment you show any vulnerability or challenge the hierarchy, that "respect" can be ripped away.

2. Money: Gangs promise quick cash—whether through selling drugs, robberies, or other illegal activities. And for some, the appeal of fast money can be too strong to resist, especially when poverty is a constant pressure. But the reality is, very few people in gangs ever get rich. Most end up constantly looking over their shoulder, spending more time running from the law than enjoying their so-called wealth. And for those who do manage to make money, it often comes at the cost of their freedom, their peace of mind, and, sometimes, their life.

3. Brotherhood: Gangs often present themselves as a family—offering support and loyalty that many people feel they don't get anywhere else. But the truth is, gang loyalty only goes so far. When push comes to shove, the so-called brotherhood will throw you under the bus to save themselves. Real family, real brotherhood, isn't based on how much trouble you can get into together—it's based on love, trust, and genuine care for each other's well-being. A gang will never give you the unconditional love and support that you deserve.

4. Protection: Another big reason people join gangs is for protection. If you're living in an area where violence is common,

the idea of having a crew to watch your back can be tempting. But here's the thing: gangs don't protect you. They put a target on your back. The moment you become affiliated with a gang, you're no longer just protecting yourself from random danger—you're part of a bigger game. You inherit the enemies of your gang, and you're constantly under threat from rival gangs, law enforcement, and even your own group if you step out of line.

The Emotional and Mental Toll of Gang Life

Now, let's talk about something that doesn't get as much attention: the emotional and mental impact of being involved in gang activity. Life in a gang is often chaotic, unpredictable, and full of stress. Even though people rarely talk about it, the mental toll is huge.

1. Living in Constant Fear: When you're in a gang, you're always on edge. You're constantly watching your back—whether it's from rival gangs, the police, or even people within your own circle. That kind of fear isn't just exhausting—it's traumatic. Living in a constant state of alertness and stress takes a serious toll on your mental health. Over time, this fear can manifest as anxiety, paranoia, or even depression. You might not feel it right away, but eventually, the weight of always being ready for danger will start to wear you down.

2. Losing a Sense of Purpose: Many people turn to gangs because they feel directionless—they're searching for something to give their life meaning. But the reality is, gangs don't give you purpose—they rob you of it. Instead of building a future you can be

proud of, gang life traps you in a cycle of violence and destruction. It can feel like there's no way out, no room to grow or achieve anything outside of the gang's control.

3. Post-Traumatic Stress: It's not talked about enough, but many people in gangs suffer from post-traumatic stress disorder (PTSD). When you're constantly exposed to violence, trauma becomes part of your daily life. Seeing friends get hurt or killed, being in dangerous situations, or even being the one committing violent acts takes a toll on your mind. You might start to feel numb, disconnected from reality, or haunted by nightmares and flashbacks. This kind of psychological trauma can stay with you long after you've left the streets.

The Legal Consequences: Losing Your Freedom

Another huge cost of gang life is the risk of losing your freedom. And this is real—law enforcement takes gang activity seriously. Once you're involved in criminal activity, you're on the radar. And the more you do, the more they build a case against you.

1. Prison Time: Many young people involved in gangs end up spending the best years of their lives behind bars. When you're locked up, the world keeps moving, but your life stands still. You miss out on opportunities, relationships, and the chance to build a future. Not to mention, life inside prison isn't easy. You're trapped in a system that's designed to keep you down, surrounded by violence, and cut off from the people who care about you.

2. Criminal Record: Even if you don't end up doing serious time, a criminal record can haunt you for the rest of your life. It makes it harder to get a job, find housing, or even go back to school. A single mistake can close doors that might have been open to you otherwise. Employers and colleges don't want to take a chance on someone with a record, no matter how much potential you have.

3. Probation and Parole: If you're lucky enough to avoid prison, you might end up on probation or parole. But here's the thing—probation and parole are still forms of control. You have to follow strict rules, check in with officers, and be constantly monitored. One slip-up, one minor mistake, and you could end up behind bars anyway.

Broken Relationships: The Personal Cost

When we think about the cost of gang life, we often focus on the individual—what it does to your body, your mind, and your future. But let's not forget the toll it takes on the people who love you. Gangs don't just hurt the person involved—they hurt everyone around them.

1. Family: Whether you realize it or not, your family bears the brunt of your choices. They worry every time you leave the house, fearing that they might get a phone call saying you've been arrested—or worse, that something tragic has happened to you. Gangs often isolate people from their families, making it harder to maintain those relationships. You might start to distance yourself from the people who care about you because they don't approve of

your lifestyle, or you might find it hard to face them knowing what you're involved in.

2. Friends: True friends want the best for you, but when you're in a gang, it can be hard to maintain those friendships. Gangs often demand loyalty above all else, forcing you to choose between your gang family and your real friends. You might end up losing people who care about you because they don't want to get caught up in your dangerous lifestyle.

3. Romantic Relationships: Being in a gang can also make it hard to build healthy romantic relationships. The chaos and instability of gang life don't leave much room for trust or emotional vulnerability. Plus, the constant threat of violence or legal trouble makes it difficult to focus on building a future with someone else.

What's the Real Payoff?

At the end of the day, what do you really get from gang life? Sure, you might have moments of feeling powerful, of getting fast money, of belonging to something bigger than yourself. But those moments are short-lived. What you lose in return—your freedom, your peace of mind, your relationships—is so much greater.

When you step back and look at the bigger picture, the scales just don't balance. The streets might give you a quick rush, but they will never offer you long-term stability, success, or happiness.

That's why it's so important to start thinking about your future now—before it's too late.

The Power of Second Chances

Here's the thing: no matter where you're at in life, no matter what choices you've made, it's never too late to turn things around. I know that leaving gang life behind is hard—it takes strength, determination, and support. But it's possible. People do it every day.

The first step is recognizing that you deserve better. You deserve a future where you're free to chase your dreams without looking over your shoulder. You deserve relationships built on love and respect, not fear and control. And you deserve the peace of mind that comes from living a life that aligns with your values.

There are resources out there to help you make that transition from gang life to a better future. Whether it's community organizations, mentors, or programs that focus on helping at-risk youth, there are people who want to see you succeed. But it all starts with a decision—the decision to choose yourself, your future, and your life over the temporary rush that gang life offers.

Rebuilding Your Life: It's Not Too Late

One of the hardest parts about walking away from a gang is the fear that it's too late—that you're too deep in, that there's no way out, or that no one will give you a second chance. I'm here to tell you that's not true. There is always a way out, and there's always a chance to rebuild.

1. Start with Self-Reflection: The first step in changing your path is looking inward. Take a hard, honest look at your life and ask yourself where you want to be in 5, 10, or 20 years. Do you

want to be locked up, running from your problems, or dealing with the constant stress of gang life? Or do you want to be free—free to build a life where you control your destiny? Reflection is powerful because it helps you see the bigger picture. You can begin to separate the immediate pressure and fear from what truly matters in the long run.

2. Find Positive Role Models: It's so important to have people in your life who can guide you in the right direction. Look for mentors—whether it's a coach, a teacher, a family member, or someone in your community—who have been where you are and who understand your struggles but have chosen a different path. They can offer advice, support, and the kind of guidance that can help you stay focused when things get tough.

3. Surround Yourself with Positive Influences: You've heard it said a thousand times, but it's true—you are who you hang around. If everyone around you is involved in gangs, violence, or illegal activity, it's nearly impossible to pull yourself out of that environment. But when you surround yourself with positive, goal-oriented people, it becomes easier to change your direction. Find a new crew—people who are hustling for success in a positive way, who have your back without dragging you into danger.

4. Education and Skills Development: One of the most powerful tools you have is knowledge. The more you learn, the more options

you have. Whether it's going back to school, enrolling in a trade program, or learning new skills, education opens doors that gang life keeps locked. And don't think that just because you've made mistakes in the past, those doors are closed to you. There are programs out there specifically for people who are trying to make a fresh start, and they want to see you succeed.

5. Work on Your Mental Health: Leaving gang life isn't just about avoiding trouble—it's about healing. The emotional scars left by years of violence, stress, and trauma don't just disappear. If you're serious about building a better future, you need to take care of your mental and emotional health. This might mean talking to a counselor, joining a support group, or just finding healthy ways to cope with stress and anxiety. Remember, asking for help isn't a sign of weakness—it's a sign of strength.

6. Build New Goals: Once you've decided to leave the streets behind, you need to focus on what you're moving toward. It's not enough to just want to avoid prison or stay out of trouble—you need something to strive for. Set goals that are meaningful to you. Do you want to start your own business, get a college degree, or become a community leader? Whatever your dream is, write it down, plan it out, and work toward it every day.

The Power of Community: Giving Back

One of the most important things you can do after leaving a gang is to give back to your community. You've been through things that many people can't understand, but your experiences can help others avoid the same mistakes.

1. Be a Mentor: Remember how we talked about the importance of finding positive role models? Well, once you've made it to the other side, you can be that role model for someone else. Young people in your community need to see that it's possible to break free from the streets, and your story can inspire them to choose a different path. Whether it's volunteering at local schools, working with community programs, or just being a positive influence to those around you, you can make a difference.

2. Get Involved in Community Programs: There are many organizations out there that are working to prevent gang involvement, support at-risk youth, and help people transition out of gang life. By getting involved, you can not only help others but also continue to build your own sense of purpose and belonging. When you dedicate your time to helping others, you strengthen your own commitment to living a positive, fulfilling life.

3. Challenge the System: Gang life is often a response to deeper, systemic problems—poverty, racism, lack of opportunities, and broken communities. As someone who has lived through these challenges, you have a unique perspective on what needs to change. Get involved in activism, speak out against injustice, and work to create real, lasting change in your community. When you use your voice and your experiences to fight for something bigger than

yourself, you become part of a movement that can change the world.

A Future Worth Fighting For

I know it's not easy. I know the streets don't let go without a fight. But here's the truth—your life is worth fighting for. You are made to lead, to rise above the violence, and to create a future that you can be proud of. The streets will always be there, but they don't have to define you. You have the power to choose a different path, a path that leads to success, happiness, and real freedom.

And once you make that choice—once you decide that you're worth more than the lies gangs tell you—the possibilities are endless. You can build a life that's full of love, respect, and purpose. You can achieve things that you never thought were possible. You can be the leader that your community needs, the role model that others look up to, and the person who proves that it's never too late to turn things around.

Your Journey Begins Now

It all starts with one decision. You've read this far because somewhere inside, you know that there's more for you than what the streets offer. You're ready to take that first step toward a brighter future, and I'm here to tell you that you can do it.

Leaving gang life is hard, but it's not impossible. With the right support, the right mindset, and the belief in yourself, you can break free from the chains that are holding you back. You can build a future that's not only free from violence and fear but full of success, love, and fulfillment.

So, are you ready to take that first step? Are you ready to claim the life you deserve?

Let's get started.

Chapter 8: The Strength to Stand Alone

81

Chapter 8: The Strength to Stand Alone

As I've walked you through the dangers and false
promises of gang life, and the many ways to pull yourself out of that trap, it's time to talk about something that's crucial to your journey—the strength to stand alone.

Standing alone isn't about being isolated or lonely. It's about finding the inner strength to stick to your values, your vision, and your dreams, even when it feels like the whole world is against you. It's about resisting the pressure that tells you to fall in line with what everyone else is doing. And believe me, that pressure can be overwhelming, especially when you're surrounded by a culture that glorifies the very things you're trying to escape from.

In this chapter, we're going to dig deep into what it takes to stand tall when it feels like no one's got your back, when it feels like the streets are pulling you in, and when it feels like your friends and even your family don't understand why you're trying to change.

Why It's So Hard to Stand Alone

Before we get into how you can develop the strength to stand alone, we need to talk about why it's so hard in the first place. When you grow up in environments where gangs, violence, and illegal activity are seen as normal, or even something to be proud of, trying to separate yourself can feel like you're turning your back on everything you've ever known. There's a deep sense of loyalty to the streets, to your crew, to the people you've been through struggles with. Walking away from that doesn't just feel like a personal decision—it feels like you're abandoning your past, your identity, and even your people.

But here's the thing: loyalty doesn't mean sacrificing your future for someone else's mistakes. Loyalty doesn't mean staying stuck in a life that will only lead to jail, death, or misery. Real loyalty is about standing by the values and principles that will lift you and your community up—not tear you both down.

You've probably heard people say, "It's just the way it is." You hear this a lot when it comes to gang life or street violence. It's like people accept that there's no other option, that this is just how life is supposed to be. But I'm telling you now: That's a lie. It's a lie that keeps us trapped in cycles of violence, poverty, and pain. Breaking free from that lie takes real strength, and that strength comes from within.

Facing the Pressure

Peer pressure is real, and it's relentless. When everyone around you is living a certain way, it's hard to be the one to say, "I'm not going to do that anymore." People will challenge you. They'll laugh at you. They'll call you soft, a sellout, or worse. Sometimes, it's not even words—it's just that look, that feeling you get when people are watching you, waiting for you to slip up or come crawling back.

I won't sugarcoat it: that pressure is going to test you in ways you can't imagine. Walking away from a gang or a life in the streets is like walking away from everything you know, everything you've been told will make you respected, make you feared, make you somebody. But standing alone is about realizing that none of that is real power. Real power is in your ability to say no. Real power is in your ability to choose your future, even when no one else around you believes you can.

Here's the reality: the pressure will never completely go away. Even after you've made the decision to turn your life around, there will be days when you'll feel tempted to go back. Maybe it's because you're frustrated. Maybe you've hit a roadblock on your new path, and it feels easier to go back to what's familiar. Or maybe it's just because you miss the camaraderie, the sense of belonging that gang life gave you.

This is why building mental resilience is so important. You have to train your mind to withstand the pressure, just like you would train your body to withstand physical pain or exhaustion. Every time you resist the urge to go back, every time you stand firm in your decision to build a better life, you get stronger.

Choosing Yourself First

There's this idea that choosing yourself is selfish. We're taught, especially in gang culture, that loyalty to others is everything. That you have to put your crew, your gang, or your block before yourself. But I want you to flip that thinking on its head for a second. Because choosing yourself isn't selfish—it's necessary.

When you decide to choose yourself first, you're not saying that you don't care about your community or the people in your life. What you're saying is that you care enough about your future to make decisions that are going to lead to growth, success, and stability. And once you're in a better position, once you've built a life that's free from the destructive influences of the streets, that's when you can give back in a way that truly matters.

Choosing yourself first means:

Prioritizing your mental and physical health. It's impossible to build a strong, successful future if you're constantly dealing with trauma, stress, or health issues. Walking away from a life of violence or crime is the first step toward healing, but it's not the last. You have to take active steps to take care of yourself, whether that means seeking counseling, surrounding yourself with positive influences, or getting involved in activities that are good for your mind and body.

Focusing on your education and skill-building. One of the most important things you can do to stand alone is to invest in your own growth. Whether that means going back to school, learning a trade, or picking up new skills, your future depends on your ability to continually improve yourself. The more knowledge and skills you have, the more options you have in life. And when you have options, you don't feel trapped or forced into the streets.

Building your future goals. You need to have a clear vision of what you want out of life. Without goals, it's easy to drift back into old habits or allow yourself to be pulled into situations that don't serve you. When you know what you want, and you're actively working toward it, it becomes easier to resist the pull of the streets. You're not just walking away from something—you're walking toward something better.

Facing Isolation

One of the hardest parts of standing alone is dealing with isolation. When you leave a gang or start making moves to better yourself, there will be moments where you feel like you're on your own. Old friends might turn their backs on you. Family members might not understand why you're changing. And in those quiet moments, when it feels like no one is in your corner, it's easy to question your decision.

But I'm telling you now: that isolation won't last forever. It's temporary. As you start to build a new life, you'll find new people who share your vision. You'll find mentors, friends, and allies who are on the same path. But to get there, you have to be willing to go through that period of isolation, where it's just you and your dreams.

Use that time to focus on yourself. In those quiet moments, when you feel alone, that's when you grow the most. That's when you find out what you're really made of. It's in those moments that you discover your true strength. Because if you can stand alone in the face of all that pressure, if you can keep moving forward when it feels like no one is with you, then there's nothing that can stop you.

The Power of Discipline

Standing alone requires more than just mental strength—it requires discipline. You need the discipline to stick to your decisions, even when things get hard. And trust me, they will get hard. There will be setbacks, obstacles, and moments where you feel like giving up. But discipline is what separates those who succeed from those who fall back into old patterns.

Create a routine. Having a daily routine helps you stay focused and keeps your mind from wandering back to the streets. Whether it's waking up at a certain time, exercising, studying, or working, having structure in your day gives you a sense of control. It's harder to get pulled into negativity when you're focused on positive actions.

Hold yourself accountable. You have to be your own biggest supporter and toughest critic. When you slip up, acknowledge it, but don't dwell on it. Learn from it, and keep pushing forward. No one is perfect, and you're going to make mistakes. But it's how you bounce back that matters. Keep yourself accountable by setting goals and regularly checking in with yourself to see if you're on track.

Find strength in small victories. Every time you resist the temptation to go back to the streets, every time you make a positive decision, that's a victory. Celebrate those moments. It's easy to get discouraged if you're only focused on the end goal, but real success is built on small, consistent wins. The more you acknowledge your progress, the more motivated you'll be to keep going.

Becoming a Leader

The journey of standing alone ultimately leads to something greater—it leads to leadership. When you've developed the strength to stand on your own, you become someone others look up to. You become a leader, not just in your own life, but in your community.

People will see the changes you've made, and they'll want to know how you did it. They'll see that you've found a way out of the cycle of violence and destruction, and they'll come to you for guidance. This is where your power to truly make a difference comes into play. By becoming a leader, you're not just transforming your own life—you're becoming a role model for others who are still trapped in the life you left behind. You become proof that change is possible.

When you stand alone and succeed, you set an example that others can follow. And I'm not just talking about people in your neighborhood. You become a symbol of hope for all the young people who feel like they have no way out, like they're stuck in a system that's designed to keep them down. When they see someone like you—someone who's walked the same streets, faced the same challenges, and made it out—they start to believe that maybe they can do it too.

How to Lead Without a Gang

Leadership doesn't mean having a crew or a gang of people following your every move. Real leadership is about influencing others through your actions and your mindset. It's about standing firm in your values, no matter how hard the pressure gets. And here's the truth: you don't need a gang to be a leader.

The streets will tell you that the only way to gain respect is through fear and intimidation. But the reality is, true respect comes from integrity, from staying true to your word, and from lifting others up instead of tearing them down. When you lead with integrity, people will naturally gravitate toward you—not because they fear you, but because they trust you.

Leadership is about guiding others through the example you set. It's about showing others that there's more to life than the streets, that there's a better way. And you don't need a title or a position to do that. You just need to live your life in a way that reflects the values and principles you believe in.

The Ripple Effect

One of the most powerful things about standing alone and becoming a leader is the ripple effect it creates. When you make the decision to turn your life around, you inspire others to do the same. Maybe it's your younger sibling who looks up to you. Maybe it's your friends who are still caught up in the gang life, but who see you breaking free. Or maybe it's someone you don't even know, someone who's watching from a distance, taking note of your transformation.

Every positive step you take sends a message to the people around you: that change is possible, that they can make it out too. And that's how real change happens—not just for you, but for your entire community.

Final Thoughts

As you walk the path of standing alone, you'll discover that it's not really about being alone at all. It's about finding your inner strength, your purpose, and your direction. It's about discovering who you really are, free from the influence of the streets or anyone else who tries to control your destiny.

And once you find that strength, once you stand firm in your decision to build a better life, you'll realize that you were never truly alone. You'll have a network of people—mentors, friends, and even strangers—who will support you on your journey. You'll find a community of like-minded individuals who share your vision for a brighter future.

So, as you move forward, remember this: Standing alone is just the first step toward building something greater. It's the foundation for a life of purpose, integrity, and success. It's the path to leadership, to inspiring others, and to leaving a legacy that will outlast any gang, any street, and any temporary fame or power the streets promised you.

In the end, you were made to lead. Not by force, not by fear, but by example. And that, my friend, is the kind of leadership that changes the world.

Chapter 9: Breaking Free from the System

One of the biggest challenges you'll face on your journey out of gang life and into true leadership is learning how to break free from the system—the larger system that has, for so long, held you and so many others back. By "system," I mean the complex network of economic, social, and institutional barriers that exist in our world, making it harder for people—especially Black youth like you—to thrive. Whether it's the school-to-prison pipeline, lack of economic opportunities, or the justice system itself, these forces are often working against you from the start.

This chapter is about understanding the system for what it is, recognizing its traps, and learning how to navigate around them. More than that, it's about breaking free from the mental, emotional, and societal chains that try to keep you confined to a life you're destined to outgrow.

Understanding the System

To break free from the system, you first have to understand how it works. This system didn't just appear out of nowhere; it's been built over generations, reinforced by laws, policies, and cultural norms that prioritize power and wealth for a select few while keeping others—especially Black and marginalized communities—oppressed and in survival mode. This isn't a conspiracy theory; it's history, and it's reality.

Here's what you need to know:

The School-to-Prison Pipeline: One of the earliest ways the system targets Black youth is through the educational system. Schools in many predominantly Black communities are underfunded, overcrowded, and often fail to provide the support and resources students need to succeed. Instead of receiving proper guidance and opportunities to learn, young Black students are disproportionately disciplined, suspended, or even expelled. For some, this early disciplinary action sets them on a path toward the criminal justice system. Once you're in that system, it becomes much harder to escape it.

The Justice System: It's no secret that the criminal justice system disproportionately targets and incarcerates Black men and boys. From biased policing practices to harsher sentencing for the same crimes committed by people of different races, the system is designed to keep young Black men behind bars. And once you're in, it's hard to get out. A criminal record can limit your opportunities for employment, housing, and even education, creating a cycle that's hard to break.

Economic Barriers: Even outside of the criminal justice system, there are economic barriers that make it difficult for Black youth to escape the conditions that often lead to gang involvement in the first place. Lack of job opportunities, inadequate access to quality education, and systemic discrimination in hiring and promotions all play a role in creating an environment where joining a gang can seem like the only viable option for survival.

Media and Cultural Influences: The media often glamorizes gang culture, making it seem like a path to respect, power, and wealth. But that's an illusion. The reality is that most people involved in gangs either end up dead or in prison, and the few who do make it out alive often suffer from lifelong trauma. The system, through media and entertainment, reinforces these destructive ideas, making it seem like there's no alternative.

By understanding how these different elements of the system work together to keep you trapped, you can start to see how you might be able to break free.

Rejecting the Labels

One of the most powerful tools the system uses to keep people down is labels. Once you've been labeled a certain way, it's hard to shake that image in the eyes of society. Whether you're labeled as a troublemaker, a dropout, a criminal, or a gang member, these labels can stick with you for life—if you let them.

But here's the thing: you are not the labels that society gives you. You are more than your mistakes, more than your circumstances, more than what people see when they look at you from the outside. Breaking free from the system starts with rejecting the labels that have been placed on you and defining yourself on your own terms.

This is where self-empowerment comes into play. You have to believe that you're more than what the world says you are. You have to believe that your future is not defined by your past, that you can rewrite your story at any moment. Once you start to see yourself as capable, worthy, and deserving of success, you begin to create opportunities for yourself that others can't take away.

Reject the label of failure. Too many young Black people are told, either directly or indirectly, that they won't amount to anything. But failure is not an identity—it's an experience, and every experience offers a chance to learn and grow.

The Power of Education

One of the most important steps in breaking free from the system is embracing education. I'm not just talking about school—though formal education is important, especially if you have the opportunity to pursue it. I'm also talking about educating yourself in every way possible: about life, about business, about the system, and about your own potential.

When you start to educate yourself, you begin to see the world differently. You begin to understand how the system works, and more importantly, how to work around it. Knowledge is power, and the more you know, the more power you have to change your circumstances.

Here's how education helps you break free from the system:

1. It opens doors: Whether it's a high school diploma, a trade certificate, or a college degree, education opens doors to opportunities that would otherwise be closed. Even if school wasn't your thing in the past, it's never too late to go back and learn. There are so many ways to educate yourself now, from online courses to community programs. Every bit of knowledge you gain is another tool in your toolbox for building a better life.

2. It changes your mindset: When you start learning new things, you start seeing new possibilities. Education helps you develop a mindset of growth and resilience. Instead of seeing obstacles as insurmountable, you start seeing them as challenges you can overcome.

3. It gives you options: One of the main reasons people stay trapped in the system is because they don't see any other options. Education expands your horizon and shows you that there are other ways to live, other ways to succeed. The more you know, the more choices you have.

4. It makes you a leader: As you educate yourself and break free from the system, you become a role model for others. People will see you making positive changes, and they'll want to know how they can do the same. By educating yourself, you position yourself to lead others out of the system as well.

Building a Support System

It's hard to break free from the system on your own. That's why it's so important to build a support system—a network of people who believe in you, who want to see you succeed, and who will help you along the way.

This support system doesn't have to be huge. In fact, it's better if it's small and filled with people you can truly trust. Maybe it's a mentor, a family member, a coach, or a teacher who sees your potential. Maybe it's a friend who's also trying to turn their life around. Whoever it is, these are the people who will keep you accountable and remind you of your goals when the system tries to pull you back in.

Find a mentor: A mentor is someone who has been where you are and can help guide you to where you want to go. They can offer advice, support, and connections that can make a huge difference in your journey. Don't be afraid to reach out to someone you admire and ask for their help.

Surround yourself with positivity: Cut out the negative influences in your life—people who are still caught up in the streets, who don't believe in your potential, or who try to drag you back into old habits. Instead, surround yourself with people who are on a similar path to success, who encourage you to keep going when things get tough.

Stay connected to your community: While it's important to leave behind the negative aspects of your old life, it's also important to stay connected to your community in a positive way. You can be a source of strength and leadership for others who are still struggling to break free from the system. This can give you a sense of purpose and remind you why you're working so hard to create a better life.

Financial Independence

A key part of breaking free from the system is achieving financial independence. One of the reasons so many young people get involved in gangs is because they don't see any other way to make money. The system makes it hard for Black youth to find legitimate work, and even when they do, the pay is often too low to make a real difference. But financial independence isn't just about making money—it's about learning how to manage the money you have, create multiple streams of income, and build long-term wealth.

Here's how you can start to achieve financial independence:

1. Learn about money: One of the reasons people stay trapped in poverty is because they don't understand how money works. Take the time to learn about budgeting, saving, investing, and building credit. These are skills that will serve you for the rest of your life.

2. Start small: You don't need a lot of money to start building financial independence. Start by saving a little bit from every paycheck or hustling in a positive way (legitimate side jobs, learning trades, etc.). Even small amounts can add up over time.

3. Build a side hustle: Whether it's cutting hair, selling clothes, or starting a YouTube channel, find a way to make money that's legal and aligns with your interests. A side hustle is a great way to earn extra income while you're working toward bigger goals. It also

gives you control over your own money and allows you to build something for yourself. The key is to start small and scale it up over time. Once you gain momentum and see results, your confidence in your ability to make money outside the system will grow.

4. Invest in your future: Once you start earning money, it's important to think about the future. Don't just live for today—invest in things that will grow over time and secure your financial independence for years to come. This could mean learning about stocks, real estate, or starting a business. The earlier you start thinking long-term, the more options you'll have down the road.

5. Avoid debt traps: One of the ways the system keeps people financially enslaved is through debt. It's easy to get caught up in payday loans, credit card debt, or other predatory financial schemes that target people who are already struggling. Stay vigilant about debt, and learn how to use credit wisely. Avoid borrowing money unless it's for something that will build your future, like education or a business investment.

6. Think entrepreneurially: One of the best ways to achieve financial independence is to think like an entrepreneur. Instead of relying on a traditional job to pay the bills, explore ways you can create opportunities for yourself. This could mean starting your own business, freelancing, or investing in your skills to open new doors. Entrepreneurship gives you freedom, and it's a powerful way

to break free from the economic constraints the system places on you.

Mental and Emotional Liberation

Breaking free from the system isn't just about physical and financial independence; it's also about mental and emotional liberation. The system works hard to make you feel powerless, to make you believe that no matter what you do, you'll never succeed. This mindset can be just as dangerous as any external barrier, and overcoming it is one of the most important parts of your journey.

Here's how you can liberate yourself mentally and emotionally:

1. Change your mindset: The system conditions many people to believe that they'll never rise above their circumstances. This negative mindset can become a self-fulfilling prophecy if you're not careful. To break free, you have to change the way you think. Start believing in your ability to achieve great things. Surround yourself with positivity, and don't allow setbacks to define you. The more you shift your mindset toward success and abundance, the more you'll start to see those things manifest in your life.

2. Embrace emotional intelligence: Understanding and managing your emotions is a critical part of breaking free from the system. Life will throw challenges your way, and people will try to provoke you, but learning how to control your emotional responses is key to staying focused on your goals. Emotional intelligence involves recognizing your feelings, controlling impulsive reactions, and finding productive ways to handle stress. When you master your emotions, you become harder to manipulate and control.

3. Practice self-care: The journey to breaking free from the system can be exhausting, both mentally and physically. It's essential to take care of yourself along the way. Whether it's exercising, meditating, spending time with loved ones, or finding creative outlets, self-care will keep you grounded and motivated. You deserve to feel good about yourself, no matter what stage of the journey you're in.

4. Seek therapy if needed: Don't underestimate the power of professional help. Therapy or counseling can provide you with tools to cope with past trauma, deal with stress, and work through any emotional baggage that's holding you back. It's a sign of strength to ask for help when you need it, and mental health support can be an invaluable resource on your journey.

Building a Legacy

As you continue on your journey to break free from the system, it's important to think about the legacy you want to leave behind. When you break out of the cycle of gang life, poverty, or systemic oppression, you're not just changing your own life—you're changing the lives of future generations. Your choices today will create a ripple effect that impacts your family, your community, and the world.

Here's how you can start building a legacy that lasts:

1. Pay it forward: Once you've gained some stability and success, think about how you can help others who are still struggling. Whether it's through mentorship, volunteering, or simply sharing your story, your experience can inspire and guide others. You can be a source of hope for someone else who feels trapped in the same way you once did.

2. Create generational wealth: Financial independence is about more than just making money for yourself—it's about building wealth that can be passed down to future generations. Start thinking about how you can invest in things that will provide long-term financial security for your children, your family, or your community. Real estate, business ownership, and investments in education are all ways to build generational wealth.

3. Become a leader in your community: Once you've broken free from the system, you have a unique perspective that can help your community. Whether you run for local office, start a community organization, or simply use your voice to advocate for change, leadership is one of the most powerful ways to make an impact. You've already shown the strength and courage to break free from the system—now it's time to lead others in doing the same.

4. Leave a positive mark on the world: Your life has the potential to influence more people than you can even imagine. By staying true to your values, working hard, and helping others, you create a ripple effect that can extend far beyond your immediate circle. Think about the bigger picture and the mark you want to leave on the world. You don't have to be famous to make a difference; the impact you make on the lives of those around you is enough to change the world in ways you may never fully see.

Conclusion: Breaking Free for Good

Breaking free from the system is not an easy task, but it's possible. The system may be designed to hold you down, but you have the power to rise above it. You have the strength, the intelligence, and the resilience to carve out your own path. The system is a complex web of barriers, but the key to freedom lies within you—through your education, your mindset, your financial independence, and your ability to lead others.

Every day you make the choice to live differently, you're taking a step toward breaking free. And every step you take, you're not only changing your own life—you're paving the way for others to do the same. You're showing the world that you were made to lead, and that no system, no gang, no stereotype can define who you are or who you will become.

This journey is long, and it will be hard at times, but never forget: you are not alone. There are people who believe in you, who want to see you succeed, and who will support you every step of the way. The system may be strong, but you are stronger. You have the power to break free for good, and when you do, you'll look back and realize that all the struggles, all the sacrifices, were worth it.

Your future is yours to create. Now, go out and lead the way.

Chapter 10: Resources and Support: Programs and Organizations to Help You Thrive

As we move forward in this journey of breaking free from the streets and avoiding the pitfalls of gang life, it's essential to recognize that you don't have to do it alone. There are countless programs, organizations, and support systems specifically designed to help youth at risk of gang violence or those who are trying to escape a gang lifestyle. These resources exist to provide guidance, mentorship, and practical tools to help you create a new path. Whether you need emotional support, job training, legal advice, or simply someone to talk to, there's help available.

In this chapter, we're going to dive deep into the importance of finding support and utilizing the resources that can help you succeed. We'll also explore specific organizations and hotlines that are available to you right now, so you know exactly where to turn if you need help.

Why Support Systems Matter

No matter how strong or determined you are, the process of leaving a gang or avoiding gang involvement requires more than just individual willpower. It requires access to the right support systems—people and programs that can guide you, encourage you, and provide the resources you need to make lasting changes.

A strong support system can offer:

Guidance and mentorship: Having someone who has been through similar struggles can be invaluable. Mentors provide insight, advice, and emotional support, helping you navigate your way out of the streets and toward a better future.

Practical resources: Many organizations offer job training, educational programs, and counseling to help you build a new life.

They can also provide connections to employers, schools, and other opportunities that may not be available otherwise.

Legal assistance: If you're dealing with legal issues related to gang activity, there are organizations that can offer free or low-cost legal help. These resources can help you navigate the court system, understand your rights, and work toward clearing your record.

Emotional and psychological support: Leaving a gang or overcoming the influence of the streets can be an emotionally intense experience. Support groups, counseling services, and mental health programs can help you deal with trauma, stress, and the emotional toll of the process.

Organizations and Resources for At-Risk Youth and Ex-Gang Members

Now, let's take a look at some specific programs and organizations that are dedicated to helping at-risk youth and former gang members. These groups have a proven track record of success and offer various forms of assistance, from mentorship to job training to legal help.

1. National Gang Center (NGC)

Website: www.nationalgangcenter.gov

The National Gang Center provides research, training, and technical assistance to communities trying to prevent and reduce gang-related crime. They offer resources for youth, community leaders, and law enforcement agencies. They also support programs that focus on gang prevention and intervention.

2. Cure Violence Global

Website: www.cvg.org

Cure Violence uses a public health approach to prevent and reduce violence by identifying and intervening with high-risk individuals before violence occurs. They have programs in cities across the United States and internationally, and their methods have been shown to reduce gang violence in communities.

3. Homeboy Industries

Website: www.homeboyindustries.org

Based in Los Angeles, Homeboy Industries is the largest gang intervention, rehabilitation, and re-entry program in the world. They offer job training, education, and mental health services to former gang members and previously incarcerated individuals. Their goal is to provide hope and support to those seeking to leave behind a life of violence and criminal activity.

4. Gang Alternatives Program (GAP)
   Website: www.gangfree.org

GAP provides gang prevention and intervention services to youth and families in at-risk communities. They offer educational workshops, community engagement initiatives, and youth development programs to help young people avoid gang involvement. They also work to build bridges between law enforcement and communities to reduce gang violence.

5. Street Poets Inc.

Website: www.streetpoetsinc.com

Street Poets is a Los Angeles-based organization that uses poetry, music, and creative writing as a form of healing for at-risk youth. They offer workshops, mentoring, and community-building programs to help young people express themselves, connect with others, and stay out of gangs. Their focus is on providing emotional support and building resilience through creativity.

6. Operation Peacemaker Fellowship (Advance Peace)

Website: www.advancepeace.org

Operation Peacemaker Fellowship, part of Advance Peace, is focused on reducing gun violence and providing alternatives to gang life. They offer mentorship, life coaching, and fellowship programs to at-risk youth, with a goal of reducing violent crime and helping young people achieve success outside of gang culture.

7. The Youth Gang Prevention Fund (Canada)

Website: www.publicsafety.gc.ca

This organization provides funding for gang prevention and intervention programs across Canada, with a focus on working with young people who are at risk of joining gangs. They support initiatives that provide education, job training, and community engagement opportunities to youth.

8. Youth Advocate Programs (YAP)

Website: www.yapinc.org

YAP works with young people and their families to prevent involvement in the juvenile justice system and to reduce gang activity. They offer mentorship, education, and support services designed to help youth build positive connections with their communities and avoid violence.

9. The National Network for Safe Communities

Website: www.nnscommunities.org

This organization works with cities across the United States to reduce violence and build trust between law enforcement and communities. They focus on gang violence reduction, group violence intervention, and community reconciliation. Their programs provide support for those leaving gangs and help prevent others from getting involved in the first place.

10. Gang Intervention Services of Chicago (GISC)

Website: www.ganginterventionservices.com

GISC provides outreach, education, and intervention services for at-risk youth in Chicago. Their programs aim to prevent gang recruitment and offer alternatives to young people who might otherwise be drawn into gang culture. They also offer family support services to help create a positive environment at home.

Hotlines and Immediate Assistance

Sometimes, you need help right away, and that's where hotlines come in. These hotlines can connect you to crisis counselors, resources, and support services whenever you need them:

1. National Gang Hotline

Phone: 1-855-NO-GANGS (1-855-664-2647)

Provides support and resources for individuals looking to leave gang life or avoid gang recruitment. They can connect you to local organizations and programs designed to help you stay safe and move forward.

2. Boys Town National Hotline

Phone: 1-800-448-3000

This hotline provides 24/7 crisis counseling and support for at-risk youth and families. Whether you're struggling with violence, family issues, or emotional challenges, they can provide help and guidance.

3. National Runaway Safeline

Phone: 1-800-RUNAWAY (1-800-786-2929)

This hotline offers support for youth who are thinking about running away, or who are already on the streets. They can connect you to shelters, counseling services, and resources to keep you safe.

4. National Suicide Prevention Lifeline

Phone: 1-800-273-TALK (1-800-273-8255)

This hotline provides 24/7 support for individuals dealing with depression, suicidal thoughts, or emotional distress. Mental health struggles are common when leaving a gang, and this lifeline can provide immediate assistance.

Conclusion: The Power of Seeking Help

No matter where you are in your journey—whether you're just starting to consider leaving a gang or you've already taken steps toward a better future—there are people and organizations ready to support you. The resources listed in this chapter are just the beginning. These programs can offer the guidance, mentorship, and practical help you need to move forward with confidence.

It's important to remember that seeking help is not a sign of weakness—it's a sign of strength. It takes courage to ask for support, especially when you've been taught to handle everything on your own. But reaching out for help can be the key that unlocks the door to a new life.

Use the resources available to you, build a network of positive influences, and stay committed to your journey. The road to a better future may be challenging, but with the right support system, it's a road you can travel with hope, confidence, and determination.

Chapter 11: Stories of Transformation

In a world that often seems consumed by darkness, stories of transformation serve as powerful beacons of hope. This chapter will explore the journeys of individuals who once walked the perilous path of gang life but chose to turn their lives around. Their stories demonstrate that change is possible, highlighting the choices they made and the support they received. The experiences of Stanley "Tookie" Williams, Carlos Cruz, Antong Lucky, and Richard Cabral will serve as inspirational examples of resilience and redemption.

Stanley "Tookie" Williams: The Journey from Gang Leader to Advocate

Stanley "Tookie" Williams was a name that echoed through the streets of Los Angeles, synonymous with the gang culture he helped to create. As a co-founder of the Crips in the early 1970s, Williams was immersed in a life of violence and crime. He was involved in numerous illegal activities that ultimately led to his arrest and conviction for murder, resulting in a death sentence in 1981.

However, it was during his time on death row that Williams experienced a profound transformation. He began to reflect on the impact of his actions, not only on his life but also on the lives of countless others affected by gang violence. Williams realized that the gang lifestyle led to destruction, pain, and heartbreak, not just for individuals but for entire communities.

In a quest for redemption, Williams took steps to change his narrative. He became an advocate for peace, using his voice to educate others about the consequences of gang involvement. Williams authored several children's books, including "Life in Prison," which shared his experiences and aimed to deter youth from making the same mistakes he had. Through these writings, he emphasized the importance of making positive choices and highlighted the power of education as a tool for change.

Williams's transformation culminated in his nomination for the Nobel Peace Prize in 2001, reflecting the impact of his advocacy work. Though he was ultimately executed in 2005, his legacy lives on, inspiring countless individuals to choose a different path. Williams's story underscores the belief that even those who have made grave mistakes can find a way to contribute positively to society.

Carlos Cruz: Finding Strength in Adversity

Carlos Cruz's journey began in a neighborhood rife with gang activity. Growing up, he felt the pressure to conform and sought acceptance in a local gang. Carlos believed that gang life would offer him protection and status, but soon realized that it only brought violence and turmoil into his life. After several run-ins with the law and a period of incarceration, Carlos faced a pivotal moment of self-reflection.

While incarcerated, Carlos began to participate in educational programs that opened his eyes to new possibilities. He met mentors who encouraged him to pursue his education and to look beyond the confines of his environment. Inspired by their support, he made the decision to turn his life around.

After his release, Carlos dedicated himself to helping others who found themselves in similar situations. He became involved in community programs focused on mentorship and youth engagement, sharing his story to warn others about the dangers of gang life. Carlos founded a nonprofit organization aimed at providing resources and opportunities for at-risk youth, emphasizing the importance of education and personal development.

Carlos's transformation was fueled by his determination to break the cycle of violence that had gripped his community for far too long. He now serves as a role model for young people, illustrating that change is achievable and that one's past does not have to define their future.

Antong Lucky: A Life Reclaimed

Antong Lucky was once a high-ranking member of the Bloods in Los Angeles, deeply entrenched in a life of crime and violence. As he rose through the ranks, he witnessed the devastating consequences of gang life, including the loss of friends and family members to violence. After years of participating in gang activities, Antong faced a turning point when he was sentenced to prison for his crimes.

During his time in prison, Antong had the opportunity to reflect on his choices and the life he had been leading. He began to engage in rehabilitation programs, seeking to understand the deeper issues that had led him to join a gang in the first place. This introspection sparked a desire for change.

Upon his release, Antong dedicated his life to helping others escape the clutches of gang life. He became a mentor to at-risk youth, sharing his experiences and offering guidance to those struggling with the same temptations he once faced. Antong founded a nonprofit organization focused on gang prevention and intervention, providing resources and support for individuals seeking to leave gangs behind.

Antong's transformation is a powerful example of resilience. He demonstrates that even those who have walked the darkest paths can reclaim their lives and make a positive impact on their communities. His work continues to inspire young people to choose a different future and to understand that their circumstances do not dictate their potential.

Richard Cabral: From Gang Member to Artist and Activist

Richard Cabral's life story reflects the struggles many face in communities plagued by violence. Growing up in Los Angeles, he became involved with a gang as a teenager, believing it was the only way to earn respect and protection. However, gang life quickly led him down a destructive path filled with crime, incarceration, and despair.

After several years of involvement in gang activities, Richard faced the consequences of his choices when he was sentenced to prison. It was during this time that he began to explore his creativity through art and writing. Engaging with these forms of expression allowed Richard to process his experiences and emotions in a way he had never done before.

Upon his release, Richard committed to transforming his life through his artistic talents. He became involved in community theater and eventually earned a role in the television series "American Crime." Through his work in the arts, Richard found a platform to share his story and advocate for change in his community.

Richard's journey from gang member to artist and activist exemplifies the healing power of creativity. He now works with young people in at-risk communities, using art as a tool for expression and empowerment. Richard encourages youth to channel their experiences into creativity rather than violence, offering them an alternative path toward success and fulfillment.

The Importance of Community Support

The stories of Stanley Williams, Carlos Cruz, Antong Lucky, and Richard Cabral illustrate the transformative power of choice, resilience, and the support of community. Each individual faced unique challenges but ultimately chose to break free from the cycle of gang life.

Their journeys highlight the significance of mentorship and community resources in facilitating transformation. Whether through educational programs, artistic expression, or community engagement, the support systems they encountered played a crucial role in their ability to turn their lives around.

As you reflect on these stories, remember that change is possible. It requires courage, determination, and a willingness to seek help and support. The paths of these individuals serve as reminders that, regardless of your past, a brighter future is within reach. Together, we can forge a new narrative and inspire others to do the same.

Conclusion: The Power of Transformation

The stories of Stanley Williams, Carlos Cruz, Antong Lucky, and Richard Cabral serve as powerful testaments to the resilience of the human spirit and the capacity for change. Each individual faced the shadows of their past, grappling with the consequences of their actions while navigating the often-treacherous waters of gang life. Their journeys remind us that it is possible to break free from destructive cycles, redefine one's identity, and contribute positively to society.

Transformation does not happen overnight. It requires courage, commitment, and a support network willing to uplift and guide individuals on their new paths. The challenges faced by those seeking to leave gang life can be daunting, but these stories demonstrate that the road to redemption is achievable.

As you reflect on these narratives, consider how your choices can shape your future. The paths of these individuals show that your past does not have to dictate your present or future. You have the power to choose differently, to seek help, and to embrace a life filled with purpose and potential.

In the face of adversity, remember that you are not alone. There are organizations, mentors, and resources available to support you on your journey. Embrace the possibility of transformation and hold on to the belief that change is within your reach. The future can be brighter, not just for you but for your community as well. By making the choice to lead a different life, you can inspire others to follow suit, creating a ripple effect of positive change.

As we conclude this chapter, take these stories of transformation to heart. They are not just tales of individuals who overcame adversity; they are calls to action for all of us. Together, we can create a new narrative—one that emphasizes hope, resilience, and the power of community in fostering lasting change. Your story is still being written, and with each choice you make, you have the opportunity to transform not only your life but also the lives of those around you.

Chapter 12: Moving Forward Together

As we reach the conclusion of this book, it's crucial to reflect on the journey we've taken and the path that lies ahead. "Moving Forward Together" is not just a phrase; it embodies the spirit of community, support, and shared purpose that will empower you to create a brighter future for yourself and those around you. Throughout this journey, we've explored the importance of self-discipline, education, mentorship, and utilizing the resources available to you. Now, we'll focus on the significance of collective effort and community in achieving lasting change.

The Power of Community

When we talk about moving forward together, we need to acknowledge the power of community. Community is more than just a group of people living in the same area; it's a network of support, trust, and shared goals. For many young people caught in the cycle of gang life or facing the threats of gang violence, community can be a sanctuary, a place of healing, and a source of strength.

1. Creating a Safe Space

A community can provide a safe environment where you can express yourself without fear of judgment or violence. Safe spaces encourage open dialogue, creativity, and collaboration. In these environments, individuals feel free to share their struggles and triumphs, creating a collective resilience that can combat the negative influences that may have once surrounded them.

2. Peer Support and Shared Experiences

Connecting with others who have faced similar challenges can be incredibly empowering. Peer support allows you to share your experiences, learn from one another, and foster a sense of belonging. You're not alone in your struggles; others have walked similar paths and can offer valuable insights and encouragement. Together, you can lift each other up, share strategies for overcoming obstacles, and celebrate each other's successes.

3. Building Leadership Skills

Being part of a supportive community also provides opportunities for you to step into leadership roles. As you gain confidence and skills, you can inspire others to make positive changes in their lives. Leadership is not just about authority; it's about influence and the ability to motivate others toward common goals. When you become a leader in your community, you help create a culture of support and empowerment, encouraging others to follow suit.

The Importance of Mentorship

As we discussed in earlier chapters, mentorship is a crucial component of personal growth and success. Moving forward together means recognizing the importance of mentorship—both seeking it and offering it to others.

1. Finding a Mentor

If you're looking to move forward, consider seeking out a mentor who can guide you on your journey. A mentor can provide valuable insights based on their own experiences, offer practical advice, and help you navigate the challenges ahead. This relationship can be transformative, providing you with the encouragement and resources you need to achieve your goals.

2. Becoming a Mentor

As you grow and develop, remember the importance of giving back to your community by becoming a mentor yourself. Sharing your story and experiences with younger individuals or peers can create a ripple effect of positive change. Mentoring is a way to inspire others, provide guidance, and help them avoid the pitfalls you may have faced. By investing your time and energy in someone else's growth, you reinforce the values of support, kindness, and community.

Taking Action: Community Engagement

Moving forward together also means taking action in your community. It's about actively engaging with others to create positive change, whether through volunteering, participating in local initiatives, or starting your own projects.

1. Get Involved

Look for opportunities to get involved in community programs that focus on youth empowerment, violence prevention, or mentorship. Organizations like those mentioned in the previous chapter often seek volunteers, mentors, and advocates. Your involvement can make a real difference in the lives of others and contribute to a safer, more supportive community.

2. Start Your Own Initiative

If you see a need in your community that isn't being met, consider starting your own initiative. Whether it's a mentorship program, a youth sports league, or a creative arts project, your passion and vision can inspire others to join you. Working together toward a common goal can strengthen bonds within your community and provide meaningful experiences for everyone involved.

3. Advocate for Change

Use your voice to advocate for policies and programs that benefit at-risk youth and communities impacted by gang violence. Attend local meetings, engage with policymakers, and raise awareness about the issues that matter to you. Advocacy is a powerful tool for creating systemic change, and your efforts can contribute to a brighter future for your community.

Overcoming Obstacles Together

While the journey ahead is promising, it's essential to acknowledge that challenges will arise. Moving forward together means supporting one another through these obstacles, whether they are personal struggles, societal issues, or setbacks in your plans.

1. Facing Challenges Head-On

Understand that setbacks are a natural part of any journey. When faced with obstacles, lean on your community for support. Share your challenges with your peers, mentors, and family members. Together, you can brainstorm solutions, offer advice, and lift each other up during tough times.

2. Building Resilience

Resilience is the ability to bounce back from adversity. Developing resilience is a collective effort; it involves learning from failures, adapting to change, and remaining focused on your goals. By sharing your experiences with one another, you can cultivate a culture of resilience in your community, empowering everyone to face challenges with determination and strength.

3. Celebrating Successes

As you move forward together, remember to celebrate your successes—both big and small. Acknowledging achievements fosters a positive atmosphere and encourages continued growth. Whether it's completing a training program, reaching a personal goal, or helping someone else find their path, celebrate these moments as a community. Your successes can inspire others and reinforce the belief that change is possible.

Embracing the Future

As we conclude this journey, let's look ahead to the future. The path you choose to take is not just about you; it's about the impact you will have on others and the legacy you'll leave behind. Moving forward together means building a future where kindness, support, and empowerment are at the forefront.

1. Envisioning Your Future

Take a moment to visualize your future. What do you see? What kind of impact do you want to have on your community? By envisioning your future, you can create a roadmap that guides your decisions and actions. Setting clear goals and aspirations will keep you focused and motivated.

2. Staying Committed to Growth

Commit to lifelong learning and personal growth. The journey of self-improvement doesn't end here; it's an ongoing process. Engage with resources, seek out new opportunities, and never stop challenging yourself. By staying committed to growth, you'll be better equipped to face the challenges that come your way.

3. Inspiring Others

Remember that your journey can inspire others. Your commitment to change, resilience, and community can motivate those around you to take similar steps. By living your truth and embracing the values of support and empowerment, you'll encourage others to join you in creating a brighter future for everyone.

Conclusion: Moving Forward Together

"Moving Forward Together" is more than just a chapter; it's a call to action. It's an invitation to join hands with others who share your vision for a better future. Together, you can create a community that thrives on support, empowerment, and resilience.

As you move forward, know that you are not alone. You have the power to shape your own destiny, and by working together, you can create a ripple effect of positive change that extends far beyond yourself. The future is bright, and it's yours for the taking. Embrace the journey ahead with courage, determination, and a commitment to lift each other up as you forge new paths together.

Also by James Hardy

Made To Lead: A Guide Against Gangs For At Risk Youth

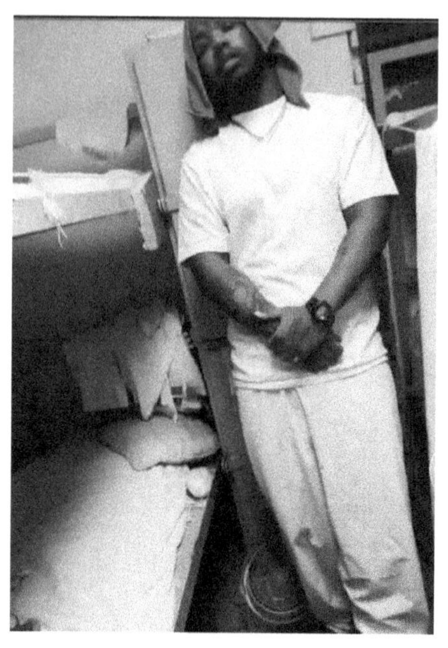

About the Author

James Hardy, known by his pseudonym "$ENT," is an emerging author hailing from the East side of Atlanta, Georgia. Hardy has captivated readers with his Urban Fiction novels, including The Pain Behind The Pole Vol 1 and Beautiful Lies, Deadly Deceptions: A Ghetto Love Affair. He also offers powerful nonfiction through his guide for at-risk youth, Made To Lead: A Guide Against Gangs For Black Youth, and brings imagination to life with the children's book Charlie's Incredible Superpower Sandwich.

Despite facing nearly a decade of incarceration, Hardy continues to write with the goal of inspiring others. As he anticipates his release, he is determined to elevate his writing career, using his own experiences and storytelling to motivate and uplift those who may be struggling. His passion for writing and commitment to creating change through his work have solidified his position as a fresh and bold voice in modern literature.